ENCOUNTERS
with
INSCRIPTIONS
a memoir

KRISTIN CZARNECKI

Legacy Book Press LLC
Camanche, Iowa

For NAK and DPK

Table of Contents

Preface

Home alone one night, I perused my Brontë shelves: a complete set of the novels from 1902; Folio Society editions of *Jane Eyre*, *Wuthering Heights*, and *The Tenant of Wildfell Hall*; an assortment of biographies; *The Brontës: A Life in Letters*; coffee table books on Haworth Parsonage; a graphic biography of Charlotte; and Isabel Greenberg's *Glass Town*, a graphic work about the Brontë sibling juvenilia—the elaborate tales Branwell, Charlotte, Emily, and Anne spun together for years about their make-believe worlds of Angria and Gondal. I have Lucasta Miller's *The Brontë Myth*, Deborah Lutz's *The Brontë Cabinet: Three Lives in Nine Objects*, and other books on Brontë lore of which fans all over the world never seem to tire. On this night, I reached for one book in particular: an edition of *Jane Eyre* and *Wuthering Heights* together that my father had given me for Christmas when I was 14 years old. It's bound in plush red leather with gold writing on the cover and gold-edged pages. Opening it, I read the inscription: *To Kristin, for her 14ᵗʰ Christmas. Read with delight and pleasure, my dear. Love, forever and ever, Dad 1983.*

Tears welled up in my eyes, for my father had recently died. Seeing his handwriting again and his lovely inscription was like getting a little "hello" from him when I least expected it, and when I most certainly needed it. I remember reading *Jane Eyre* in that volume shortly after receiving it, but it would be another ten years before I'd read *Wuthering Heights*, in a graduate course called Novels of the Brontë Sisters, which sparked my Brontë mania. My mother shared my delight and pleasure in the Brontës, and we enjoyed talking about their lives and writing. When I visited the Brontës' home, Haworth Parsonage, for the first time in June 2004,

I couldn't wait to tell her about it—especially since my friend and I happened to visit on the 150th wedding anniversary of Charlotte Brontë and Arthur Bell Nicholls. We attended a reenactment of their wedding in the church, and Haworth residents wandered about in period clothing.

My mother would have loved it. She died nine months after my father, and my husband's father had died five months before that. I was Brontë-gazing alone in the house because my husband was out of town at our sister-in-law's funeral. She passed away at age 52, just four weeks after my mother died. It had been a brutal stretch of time, and on this rainy October night, reflecting on our losses, I turned to my books for solace and distraction. And, upon seeing my father's inscription, for remembrance as well. Of the countless things I miss about my parents, exchanging and discussing books with them might be what I miss the most.

A few months later, I found myself combing through books on another night, pulling this or that from the shelves to refresh my mind on storylines, look at beautiful dustjackets, feel the heft of a book in my hands, and inhale the aroma of creamy new pages or musty old ones. I came across another book with an inscription from my parents—and then another, and another after that. Soon, I had a stack in my arms and headed to my laptop to type the inscriptions out. The books were birthday or Christmas presents spanning my entire life. Some I had read several times, others not even once.

I decided then that I would read—or reread—all these books, not necessarily in the order in which I received them. Instead, I would let the process unfold organically and turn to them as the mood struck for a particular genre or author. I would think about what I glean from each book now. I would head down rabbit holes for related research and exploration. I would try to stave off expectations and just enjoy the reading experience. At the same time, I would reflect on where I was in life when the books were given to me: a child of 12, a teenager, an adult turning 25, then 35, then 50 years old in the blink of eye. What did my parents hope I would find in these books? Or did they simply love the fact that I was a voracious reader, like they were? How fitting that the inscription in the Brontë book sent me down this path, for as Debora Lutz explains, "The Brontës were incessant inscribers, a practice copied from their father." Inscriptions accrued as books were exchanged, gifted, and passed on to others. "Charlotte wrote in her little diary of 1829 that 'once papa lent my sister Maria a book. It was an old geography book and she wrote on its blank leaf, "Papa lent me this book."' Charlotte felt a sense of awe for this textbook that had belonged to her sister, dead already for a few years," Lutz writes. She then describes a Branwell/Brontë family Bible, with its series of inscriptions recording who gave it to whom and when. "What is crucial about this Bible," Lutz explains, "why it still exists today, is not the printed text but the chain of relationships it represents, made tangible by handwriting on the page." I see a similar chain of relationships in my parents' inscriptions to me over the years.

My parents gave me the gifts of life and literature. Delving into the books from them might, I thought, allow me to commune with them once again. I longed for our comfortable language of plot, character, chapter, and stanza. Reading these books would be a nostalgic enterprise but one that would allow me to contemplate the present and look to the future as well, for as Virginia Woolf says in *A Room of One's Own*, "books continue each other, in spite of our habit of judging them separately." They reflect, respond to, and resonate with each other across time and space. They collapse the boundaries often imposed by academia and the marketplace. In their infinite variety, they make room for readers everywhere, inviting us to consider what it means to be human in a complicated world. And so my journey began.

Chapter 1

A Light in the Attic
Poems and Drawings by Shel Silverstein

To Kristin
with all our love
Merry Christmas!
1981

Before writing about *A Light in the Attic*, given to me by my parents when I was 12 years old, I need to backtrack to its predecessor, *Where the Sidewalk Ends*, which I first encountered in the fourth grade, when our class gave it as a going away present to one of our classmates, Susan Choi, whose family was moving to another state in the middle of the school year. We were happy and excited to give her a gift. Even at ten years old, we all knew Susan was special—brilliant and kind. (She would go on, unsurprisingly, to become an award-winning novelist.) We gathered around as she unwrapped her present and unveiled *Where the Sidewalk Ends*. She thanked us as she flipped through the pages, and our teacher, Mrs. Sylvester, asked her to read a poem aloud. She stood at the front of the room and read "Sarah Cynthia Sylvia Stout Would Not Take the Garbage Out," laughing as she read. "And so it piled up to the ceilings: / Coffee grounds, potato peelings, / Brown bananas, rotten peas, / Chunks of sour cottage cheese." I found it magical—the rhyming, the drawings—and when I got home from school that day, I breathlessly told my mother all about it. Never one to refuse a child begging for a book, she bought it for me, and my friend Mia and I pored over it together countless times.

I came across *A Light in the Attic* in a bookstore in Chicago over Christmas break a couple of years later, on a day when our family had taken the South Shore train from South Bend to see the decorated windows at Marshall Fields. I remember the slow shuffling of people along the sidewalk gazing in delight at the elaborate Christmas displays: scenes from *Nutcracker*, elves, Santa, ice skaters, gingerbread houses, snowmen, and the like. On those excursions, we would have lunch at Fields's famous Walnut Room, with its towering, fragrant Christmas tree. In fact, I think we may have been in the basement of Fields, which used to have a book section, when I found *A Light in the Attic*. (I vividly remember picking out a couple of Nancy Drew books there once, too.) I'm a little fuzzy on the details, though. *Were* we in Chicago? I think we must have been, because I remember my father being there, and on an ordinary day in South Bend, the entire family wouldn't have been out together browsing a bookstore. Either way, I had the book in my hands and asked my parents if they would buy it for me. No dice. But there it was a short time later under our Christmas tree. Today, it's not quite as battered and worn as my copy of *Where the Sidewalk Ends*, but it's clear that I thumbed through its pages many times.

Reading it now after many years, I revel again in Silverstein's writing, with its humor, wordplay, rollicking rhythms, and whimsical, sometimes sinister drawings that accompany the poems or, more often, play a key role. "Have Fun" depicts a girl happily swimming because "I guarantee / There are no sharks," while a giant octopus lurks just below the surface, unbeknownst to her. "Deaf Donald" incorporates drawings of a child saying "I love you" in American Sign Language. His friend, Sue, not understanding him, grows frustrated and walks out of his life forever—one of the book's many poems on miscommunication and lost opportunities. The speaker of "Something Missing" rehashes his morning routine. "I remember I put on my socks, / I remember I put on my shoes," he says, "Yet I feel there is something / I may have forgot— / What is it? What is it? . . .." Next to the poem is a drawing of a man in suitcoat, tie, and jaunty cap—but no pants.

Many of the poems explore the imaginative possibilities in seemingly mundane objects, such as "Picture Puzzle Piece." "One picture puzzle piece / Lyin' on the sidewalk," the poem begins. "One picture puzzle piece / Soakin' in the rain. / It might be a button of blue / On the coat of the woman / Who lived in a shoe. / It might be a magical bean, / Or a fold in the red / Velvet robe of a queen." We need only let our minds roam freely to create a whole out of a tantalizing part, and Silverstein's poems encourage such creativity, like "Rock 'N' Roll Band," with its motley crew of kids dreaming big: "If we were a rock 'n' roll band, / We'd travel all over the land. / We'd play and we'd sing and wear spangly things, / If we were a rock 'n' roll band." No matter that "we ain't no rock 'n' roll band, / We're just seven kids in the sand / With homemade guitars and pails and jars / And drums of potato chip cans"—they're having a ball being noisy and exuberant. A tiny lighthouse and sailboat shimmer in the distance behind them. Such details enliven every page.

"Put Something In" strikes a similar chord as "Rock 'N' Roll Band": "Draw a crazy picture, / Write a nutty poem, / . . . Put something silly in the world / That ain't been there before." A few years ago, I began painting with watercolors and drawing with colored pencils, new endeavors for me spurred by a book arts course I took at the college where I used to teach. In addition to our class projects, our professor, Daniel—my colleague and friend—gave us weekly assignments involving painting, drawing, and collaging. I took to it instantly, but I wasn't very good, I feared. Early in the semester, we went outside with our scratchbooks, behind the art building, and were told to have fun—for two hours—with chalk, spray paint, charcoal nubs, bricks, and the bits of the natural world within reach, like twigs, leaves, dirt, and rocks. I stood there looking around, feeling bewildered and intimidated. The undergrads dived right in. They sat cross-legged on the ground. They sprayed their hands with paint and made prints and swirls and lines on their books' clean white pages. They drew, glued, and collaged. I'm pretty sure matches were lit. By the end of class, my own book's first few pages reflected a haphazard, but not half-hearted, effort at creativity. I got into the spirit of things but fell flat when it came to creating anything special.

*****

Once I bought watercolors and colored pencils, I began to stretch my wings a bit. Even then, though, I struggled with self-consciousness. Although I don't particularly care for representational art, I wouldn't paint or draw unless I had an object, or a picture of something, right in front of me. I would pick up a pencil and draw and erase, draw and erase. Knowing that Daniel would be collecting our scratchbooks a couple of times during the semester, I would imagine him looking at my pages over my shoulder (something he never would have done), not unlike the way Virginia Woolf imagines the Angel in the House—that Victorian-era phantom demanding that women write in deference to patriarchal expectations—in her 1931 lecture-turned-essay, "Professions for Women." Attempting one night to draw Branwell Brontë's painting of his sisters, I kept flubbing it. I finally scribbled it out and wrote, "Not my night. Can't draw for shit." Later, after we had turned in our books and then got them back, I saw that Daniel had written a note next to mine: "You're listening to the wrong voice." His overall comment on my paintings and drawings: "Play, play, play!"

Indeed, Silverstein's poem "Put Something In" encourages us to adopt a more childlike, less inhibited frame of mind and to just enjoy the process. Along with creativity, we're reminded to value individuality above material possessions and certainly above our own vanity, sentiments expressed in "Outside or Underneath?" Two characters, Bob and Jack, take pains with their appearance. For Bob, it's a snazzy suit. For Jack, it's quality underwear. But "Tom bought a flute and a box of crayons, / Some bread and cheese and a golden pear. / And as for his suit or his underwear / He doesn't think much about them . . . or care." Who wouldn't prefer to be Tom—confident, creative, and carefree—rather than the smug and preoccupied Bob and Jack?

Overall, the poems in *A Light in the Attic* raise a lump in my throat that surely didn't arise when I read them as a child. How did I interpret "Signals" at age twelve? I don't remember. But now, as an adult settled firmly into routine, the poem poses a hard-hitting question: "When the light is green you go. / When the light is red you stop. / But what do you do / When the light turns blue / With orange and lavender spots?" Indeed, what do you do when the unexpected occurs? When something unfamiliar crosses or blocks your path? Do you freeze? Do you cower? Do you step off the curb and cross the street regardless? Do you welcome this shake-up to the familiar rhythms of daily life, or do you turn around and go home?

"Magic Carpet" culminates in a similar query. "You have a magic carpet" that can go anywhere. You only have to tell it where to go and what to do. "So will you let it take you / Where you've never been before, / Or will you buy some drapes to match / And use it / On your / Floor?" To my dismay, I've put the magic carpet on the floor many times. Yet I love to travel and have flown on that carpet as well—to England and Ireland, to loved ones in Seattle, to cherished family vacation sites in Massachusetts. My husband and I recently renewed our passports, and we have a long list of places we want to go post-pandemic. "Magic Carpet" nudges us to go for it—not just to travel but also to seize opportunities whenever or wherever they may arise, or better yet, create them ourselves and refuse to accept the mundane. Such a message evokes Mary Oliver's poem "The Summer Day," with its speaker reveling in the grace and beauty of the natural world, and with its piercing final lines: "Tell me, what is it you plan to do / With your one wild and precious life?"

*****

This question permeates *A Light in the Attic*, with its parade of children, adults, and creatures contending with fear, insecurity, vulnerability, and regret. The voice of "Never" laments risks not taken. "I've never roped a Brahma bull, / I've never fought a duel, / I've never crossed the desert / On a lop-eared, swayback mule." Never mind that such adventures aren't feasible in the first place—at least not to most people. "Sometimes I get so depressed / 'Bout what I haven't done," the speaker states. Who among us hasn't experienced a similar sense of loss or regret? Silverstein captures such sentiments again in "Fear," in which "Barnabus Browning / Was scared of drowning, / So he never would swim / Or get into a boat / Or take a bath / Or cross a moat." Instead of venturing out and living his life, he sequesters himself at home, ultimately crying so many tears "That they filled up the room / And he drowned." Lost opportunities also feature in "The Toad and the Kangaroo" as the eponymous characters delight in encountering one another and make plans for getting married and having a child endowed with their unique characteristics. They can't agree on what to name it, however—Toadaroo or Kangaroad, Rangatoo, or Kangaree—until "the Toad had no more to say, / And the Kangaroo just hopped away. / And they never married or had a child / That could jump a mountain or hop a mile. / What a loss—what a shame— / Just 'cause they couldn't agree on a name."

Silverstein's poems consider the myriad ways we hinder ourselves. "Whatif" presents the gremlins who emerge at night to plague us: "Last night, while I lay thinking here / Some Whatifs crawled inside my ear / And pranced and partied all night long / And sang their same old Whatif song: / Whatif I'm dumb in school? / Whatif they've closed the swimming pool? / Whatif I get beat up? / Whatif there's poison in my cup?" The fears cascade, one after another: parents divorcing, the onset of war, failure, sickness, and death. Morning brings a brighter outlook, but without fail, "The nightime Whatifs strike again!" Turning to this page in the book, I was startled to see a small checkmark in blue ink in the upper left-hand corner. I must have put it there. What does it mean? That at twelve years old, I was already experiencing the nightly parade of Whatifs? That some of the fears listed were my own? "Whatif I flunk that test? . . . Whatif I tear my pants? / Whatif I never learn to dance?" What if I fight with my friends, don't have the right clothes, get bullied or teased? Was I relieved to read this poem and learn that others were also lying awake worried at night? Or was I terrified at the poem's conclusion and the promise of more whatifs to come?

There's another small blue checkmark next to "The Little Boy and the Old Man," who find they have much in common: "Said the little boy, 'Sometimes I drop my spoon.' / Said the little old man, 'I do that too.'" They wet their pants, they cry, "'But worst of all,' said the boy, 'it seems / Grown-ups don't pay attention to me.' / And he felt the warmth of a wrinkled old hand. / 'I know what you mean,' said the little old man." Even at twelve, it seems, I was struck by the poignancy of this poem. The fearful child, whispering his deepest secrets. The resigned old man, laughing and nodding to ease the boy's anxieties. Is he the child's grandfather? Is he an old man on a park bench whom the child decides to confide in? It doesn't really matter how they found each other, just that they did. A question looms, though. Which is worse: experiencing confusion, fear, and loneliness for the first time or growing so accustomed to them, you can't imagine things any other way? The poem ends with the old man's loving gesture, and a friendship blossoms between two lonely souls.

*****

Perhaps most distressing to my adult sensibilities is "Cloony the Clown," who suffers the ironic misfortune of being extremely unfunny. "His shoes were too big and his hat was too small, / But he just wasn't, just wasn't funny at all." He pulls out all the stops—"a trombone to play loud silly tunes" and "a green dog and a thousand balloons"—but his props and pratfalls only elicit tears, sighs, and anger from his audience. "One day he said, 'I'll tell this town / How it feels to be an unfunny clown.' / And he told them all why he looked so sad, / And he told them all why he felt so bad. / . . . Did everyone cry? Oh no, no, no, / They laughed until they shook the trees / With 'Hah-Hah-Hahs' and 'Hee-Hee-Hees.'" Their laughter spreads far and wide, "While Cloony stood in the circus tent, / With his head drooped low and his shoulders bent. / And he said, 'THAT IS NOT WHAT I MEANT— / I'M FUNNY JUST BY ACCIDENT.' / And while the world laughed outside, / Cloony the Clown sat down and cried." This poem terrifies me. What could be more appalling than finally mustering the courage to speak your truth only to be utterly misunderstood?

In another dimension, "Cloony the Clown" could be the prototype for T. S. Eliot's "The Love Song of J. Alfred Prufrock" as Prufrock convinces himself of the doomed nature of any attempts at communication. At least Cloony tries to explain how he feels in the hopes that he might be better understood. Prufrock doesn't even try, foreseeing only humiliation and defeat. "Then how should I begin?" he asks, "And how should I presume?" People will snicker and gossip. They'll mock his clothes, his thinning hair, his scrawny limbs. They'll make assumptions about him. They'll pin him to the wall like a wiggling, struggling bug. Two people speaking to each other, he believes, will only come to ruin. "Would it have been worth while," he asks, "To have bitten off the matter with a smile, / To have squeezed the universe into a ball / To roll it towards some overwhelming question, / To say, 'I am Lazarus, come from the dead, / Come back to tell you all, I shall tell you all'— / If one, settling a pillow by her head / Should say: 'That is not what I meant at all; / That is not it, at all.'" So he becomes bashful, tentative, Hamlet's kindred spirit in his indecisiveness. Prufrock leads a bleak, circumscribed life, "measuring out [his] life in coffee spoons" and not daring to eat a peach—images tailor-made for Silverstein drawings.

Silverstein's thematic reach knowns no bounds. "Peckin" shows a bedraggled woodpecker pecking a plastic tree because there are no more real ones—a prescient depiction of environmental devastation. "Zebra Question" points to the futility of dichotomies and seeking easy answers to complex questions. "I asked the zebra," a boy says, "Are you black with white stripes? / Or white with black stripes? / And the zebra asked me, / Are you good with bad habits? / Or are you bad with good habits?" and so on, the child and zebra engaging in an angry face-off. "Gooloo" depicts a flying, crying bird living a frustrating, impossible life: "The Gooloo bird / She has no feet, / She cannot walk / Upon the street. / She cannot build / Herself a nest, / She cannot land / And take a rest." I'm unable to recapture how I must have felt reading these poems as a child. I'm sure I loved the playfulness of some, while others must have disturbed me, with their one-two punch of distressing words and images. I appreciate Silverstein's respect for children, presenting them with a vast range of complex experiences and emotions.

I'm certain my mother rather than my father picked this book out for me. It simply wouldn't have been on his radar. But I doubt she read any of the poems before wrapping it. She might have paged through it a bit and skimmed a few lines here and there, but probably no more than that. She just wanted me to get to know and enjoy poetry, which I did. Then, the book sat on a shelf unread for decades, relegated to my small collection of "children's books." Now I know better and will turn to Silverstein for the thrill of the rhyme, the clever blending of word and image, and a broad emotional landscape whose terrain I'm still exploring.

Chapter 2

A Child's Christmas in Wales
by Dylan Thomas

Christmas, 1982
To Kristin –
A wonderful Christmas
story by a great poet.
Love,
Mother and Dad

Oh, to read *A Child's Christmas in Wales* over the holidays during a pandemic, with three of our four parents deceased, my 91-year-old mother-in-law in lockdown in her retirement village six hours away, and time on our hands to reminisce about our childhood Christmases, when our families were healthy and intact, and all was right with the world. How many such thoughts, such essays, has Dylan Thomas's tender story prompted over the years? Does that make my thoughts, my essay a cliché? Maybe—or maybe not, since nostalgia is "directed to one's personal past and not the objective past," as philosopher Paula Sweeney explains. No doubt scads of people have similar childhood memories of the holidays, yet as the narrator of *A Child's Christmas in Wales* makes clear, our idiosyncratic renditions of the past possess an undeniable magic. Nevertheless, I know all about rose-colored glasses. "Although the past cannot be restored, it can be transformed in the process of remembering," writes Julia Kindt in "On Nostalgia." "It is popular knowledge that in hindsight things tend to look better than they were. Memory idealises the past." Like the narrator of *A Child's Christmas in Wales*, though, I see in my mind's eye, clear as day, the beauty and enchantment of my family's holiday traditions.

Opening Thomas's book, I read the first sentence over and over, its lyricism and poignancy piercing my heart even while its jagged rhythm puts me off-kilter: "One Christmas was so much like another, in those years around the sea-town corner now and out of all sound except the distant speaking of the voices I sometimes hear a moment before sleep, that I can never remember whether it snowed for six days and six nights when I was twelve or whether it snowed for twelve days and twelve nights when I was six." Thus begins the narrator's deep dive into his past: carousing with friends in the snow, getting scolded by a neighbor, nestling in the warmth and safety of his home at Christmastime. He recalls the women cooking and decorating, the uncles chatting and napping, and "some few small Aunts, not wanted in the kitchen, nor anywhere else for that matter, on the very edges of their chairs, poised and brittle, afraid to break, like faded cups and saucers." (As an aunt, I hope I never become so brittle and afraid to break, let alone unwanted.) He remembers the chilled, red-nosed postman crunching through the snow, the sound of church bells ringing, and the vast array of presents both Useful—the dreaded mufflers, mittens, and scratchy wool vests from the Aunts—and Useless: the coveted candy, tin soldiers, "and a painting book in which I could make the grass, the trees, the sea and the animals any colour I pleased, and still the dazzling sky-blue sheep are grazing in the red field under the rainbow-billed and pea-green birds." I love the child's unfettered imagination.

*****

At my childhood home in South Bend, Indiana, we had no visiting aunts and uncles as my mother's family was in Massachusetts, my father's in Wisconsin. It was just the five of us at home: Mom and Dad, my sister, Cynthia, and my brother, Ted—and always a cat or two. The Christmas season began with the hanging of the Advent calendar from a nail on the mantel in the den on the first of December. Each morning when I came downstairs, I would run to it and open the tiny paper door for that day, feeling a quick, thrilling jolt of surprise each time—as I would forget from year to year which picture hid behind which door—followed by a reassuring sense of their familiarity. The Advent candles stood on

14

the kitchen table in a wreath my sister had made from thick yarn, and I looked forward to the lighting of them each night at dinner.

As Christmas drew closer, our dad strung colored lights on the bare magnolia tree in our front yard and sometimes along the bushes fronting the house. Inside, we had our fragrant live tree, acquired about a week or so before Christmas. My poor dad always had a terrible time putting it up in those small, spindly metal stands in which it would lean, sway, and tip. Strategically tied string was often involved. Once the tree was up and stable, my brother and sister and I would begin decorating: first the lights, then the garlands, then the ornaments, and finally the candy canes and glittering icicles, many of which made their way into our cats' mouths and through their innards until they dangled out the other end a day or two later. The tree smelled fresh and earthy, and I couldn't wait for the sun to go down so we could get the full effect of the colorful lights—even while I lamented how quickly Christmas break was flying by. When we were small, we'd bake cookies, making extra to leave out for Santa along with a bowl of sugar for his reindeer. One year, we baked and painted ornaments made from dough.

We'd put the presents out a few days before Christmas, and my brother and I would try to guess what was in each wrapped package. We'd shake them, feel the contours, try to peek under the paper. We got pretty good at it. It was easy to tell what was a book, what was a clothing box, what was a plastic toy of some sort. Some items remained a mystery until we opened them. One year, my brother unwrapped all his presents and then wrapped them up again. He would wake me up on Christmas morning around 6:30 or 7:00, and we'd dash downstairs to check out our stockings, full of chocolate coins in gold foil, a chocolate Santa, clear plastic candy canes filled with M&Ms, a couple of small toys, and usually an orange at the bottom, elongating the stocking and rounding out the toe in a pendulous knob. (When did we give away our stockings? How could we ever have let them go?) Everyone else would then get out of bed, my parents would make coffee, and we'd settle around and take turns unwrapping presents. Our father was always a sight to behold on Christmas morning: barely awake, squinting, hair sticking up every which way, and a huge scarf around his neck.

And the presents! Our mother was a great present buyer. Some cherished gifts include a Shaun Cassidy record, my Barbie Townhouse, and the electronic games Simon, Merlin, and a hand-held Pac-Man. I remember a soft, floppy, white stuffed animal rabbit from my sister one year. I named him Tinkerbell. My brother got the hand-held Mattel football and hockey games, which I would sneak into his room to play. One year, he got skis, placed under the tree sometime during the night. When he ran downstairs and saw them, he dropped to his knees and kissed them. And our poor parents, feigning delight at the presents we got for them when we were young. Ted presented our mom with a plastic figure of a nun one year. ("I *loved* that nun," he said to me recently.) I once bought my dad Calvin Klein cologne. Preposterous. One year, my sister, a professional ballet dancer at the time, gave me a necklace with a colorful fish pendant that she'd bought in Taiwan, where her company had recently toured. And I promptly lost it—*that morning*, not twenty minutes after I opened it. We searched everywhere for it, all morning, but it must have been swept up with the piles of wrapping paper and put out with the trash. Over thirty years later, I'm still sorry about losing that necklace. After opening presents, we had breakfast and then went to Mass. Or did we go to Mass and then have breakfast? Christmas music played on the turntable or radio all day long, and special snacks were out for the duration as well.

We always had holiday dinners with the Mast family across the street, trading off each year. One year, we'd have Thanksgiving dinner at our house and Christmas dinner at theirs, and vice versa the following year. Before dinner, while the adults were finishing getting everything ready, all the kids—we three and the four Mast children—would scope out the presents. After dinner and dessert (complete with flaming plum pudding if we were at the Masts'), we'd cross the street to the other house to check out the presents over there. I vividly recall those cold dashes across the street and the fleeting moment of melancholy upon entering the dark, empty house. We'd turn on the lights, look at the presents, and then run back to the warmth and bustle of the other home. My husband has similar stories: the tree, the food, the presents, the magic of the morning, and, in his case, the visiting relatives or car trips across the city to see aunts, uncles, and grandparents. A lifetime ago, still so vivid in our minds.

*****

Recalling his past, the narrator of *A Child's Christmas in Wales* conjures a realm of high adventure fusing the primordial with the modern:

> Years and years and years ago, when I was a boy, when there were wolves in Wales, and birds the colour of red-flannel petticoats whisked past the harp-shaped hills, when we sang and wallowed all night and day in caves that smelt like Sunday afternoon in damp front farmhouse parlours and we chased, with the jawbones of deacons, the English and the bears, before the motor-car, before the wheel, before the duchess-faced horse, when we rode the daft and happy hills bareback, it snowed and snowed.

The boy he's talking to interrupts him. "It snowed last year, too," he exclaims. "I made a snowman and my brother knocked it down and I knocked my brother down and then we had tea." The narrator replies, "But that was not the same snow."

At other points in *A Child's Christmas in Wales*, the young boy listening to the older man interjects his own experiences, but they cannot compare to the elder's. As the narrator states, snow in *his* day was more exciting and alive. "Our snow was not only shaken from whitewash buckets down the sky, it came shawling out of the ground and swam and drifted out of the arms and hands and bodies of the trees." The narrator recalls church bells ringing, while the boy "only hear[s] thunder sometimes, never bells." In truth, then, was the narrator's childhood actually fairly run-of-the-mill? Is it only in the throes of nostalgia that the magic arises? Does he experience his current life as disappointing, sorrowful, or dull, leading him to remember a childhood where everything was *more*—more special, more thrilling, more intense? Sweeney tells us "nostalgia is not to be thought of as an irrational desire to re-experience but as a rational desire to take a break from the experiences of the present and to seek refuge in previously felt

17

emotions." Despite the narrator's lavish descriptions of the material world, perhaps the emotional tenor of the time is what he's really after. When my husband and I reflect on what it was like to be a kid at Christmas, aren't we seeking the feel of it, seeking "refuge in previously felt emotions"? I would say yes, especially as a dreadful 2020 slouches to an end.

What intrigues me most about *A Child's Christmas in Wales* is the narrator's uncanny experience on Christmas morning of running headlong into his doppelgänger. He builds up to it by remembering one of the coveted Useless presents: candy cigarettes. "[Y]ou put one in your mouth and you stood at the corner of the street and you waited for hours, in vain, for an old lady to scold you for smoking a cigarette, and then with a smirk you ate it." Then he would go home for breakfast and afterwards head back outside and walk down to the "forlorn sea," describing other boys and men doing the same, year after year. "Then I would be slap-dashing home," he says:

> when out of a snow-clogged side lane would come a boy the spit of myself, with a pink-tipped cigarette and the violet past of a black eye, cocky as a bullfinch, leering all to himself. I hated him on sight and sound and would be about to put my dog whistle to my lips and blow him off the face of Christmas when suddenly he, with a violet wink, put *his* whistle to *his* lips and blew so stridently, so high, so exquisitely loud, that gobbling faces, their cheeks bulged with goose, would press against their tinselled windows, the whole length of the white echoing street.

Perhaps the anecdote is the narrator's means of acknowledging the commonality of his experiences—that masses of mischievous boys ran about on Christmas day with their whistles and their candy cigarettes. (We had them, too. What on earth were our parents, and candy manufacturers, thinking?) Far from playing the hero in his own adventure, he's just another boy on the street—something the *other* boy materializing in front of him seems to understand, taunting the narrator-as-boy with his "violet wink" and deafening blast of his whistle. Hence the narrator's hatred of his doppelgänger—an omen to him then, a reminder to him now of life's sameness, of routine, of growing old.

Yet in relating the incident, the narrator says "you" did this and "you" did that. A colloquialism, no doubt, but it may also be read as the generic "you," as if he knows he's one among many and that that's all right. After all, kids need a cohort, a sense of belonging, a group of like-minded friends. Nevertheless, the incident confounds him. That sudden rush of hatred! He then tells of running back home, where "at tea the recovered Uncles would be jolly; and the ice cake loomed in the centre of the table like a marble grave"—an odd, gloomy simile for a child to seize upon, but not for an adult. The episode wraps the narrator in a memory feedback loop intertwining his current and past selves and reminding him that childhood will be over in a flash.

*****

I can appreciate the uncanny feeling of running into yourself. Every academic conference I've been to has been full of women like me: similar clothes, glasses, shoulder bags, and shoes. These women are my people, beloved to me, yet we can be spotted a mile away, a disconcerting fact driven home when I took the GRE in Chicago many years ago, before it was available online. There were about fifteen people in the room. The proctor distributing the tests called out the subject, and people would raise their hands. "History! Chemistry!" When she called, "English literature!" four of us, all young women, raised our hands, and a guy seated in front of me turned around, gave us all the once over, and said, "Gee, I never would have guessed." What gave us away? Glasses? A bun held in place with a pencil?

Even worse was interview season at MLA—the Modern Language Association's annual conference and cattle call. One year, some article, probably in the *Chronicle of Higher Education*, decreed that a saturated purple was the "in" color—sophisticated and professional—and right on cue, hundreds if not thousands of job applicants roamed the host city sporting a deep purple blouse, scarf, or necktie. The same unsettling sensation arose any time I heard my students parrot something I said. I always thought I wanted my students to listen to me and remember what I said during class. But when it came back to me verbatim in an essay, exam, or class discussion, I found it unnerving. Disappointing, somehow.

A Child's Christmas in Wales draws to a close with the narrator recalling the warm, drowsy post-meal evening as the aunts sip wine and sing, and laughter fills the room. When he gets into bed, he gazes up at the moon outside his window, looks at the lights in other people's homes, and "hear[s] the music rising from them up the long, steadily falling night. . . . I said some words to the close and holy darkness, and then I slept"—a sentence rivaling in its power and beauty the last sentence in James Joyce's "The Dead": "His soul swooned slowly as he heard the snow falling faintly through the universe and faintly falling, like the descent of their last end, upon all the living and the dead." The narrator doesn't mind going to bed, for he anticipates the sense of peace it will bring, and I imagine he must be worn out after running in and out of the house all day and after the high, sustained emotional pitch of Christmas. I can't remember if I resisted going to bed on Christmas night. Probably not. We would have been deliciously worn out, too, and I loved lying in bed looking at the colorful electric candle in my bedroom window.

I don't remember my parents talking much about their childhood Christmases, but I can guess what they must have been like, since our family traditions surely stemmed from theirs. They grew up in modest homes with siblings and, like the narrator of *A Child's Christmas in Wales*, had visiting aunts, uncles, and grandparents. I can easily picture my father outside in the snow of a Wisconsin winter, raising hell with his friends. I can envision my mother gathered around the dinner table or the tree with her parents and aunts, who were like mothers to her. I hadn't really thought about it much, but after reading *A Child's Christmas in Wales* and "attempting to purposefully trigger nostalgia," as Sweeney writes, I'm glad to have these tableaux of their young world in my mind that bring to life the few faded photographs I have of them as children. And I feel a sense of peace imagining them now in the "close and holy darkness" of eternal slumber.

Chapter 3

Reading in the Dark
by Seamus Deane

To Kristin
from Mom
Christmas 1997

I can think of several reasons why my mother might have given me *Reading in the Dark*. Seamus Deane was a professor at the University of Notre Dame, where I had gone to college and where my father was also a professor. I had recently taken a Joyce seminar in graduate school and become enamored of Irish literature. And the novel had received glowing reviews. I remember reading it in bed, my husband beside me, in our last apartment in Chicago. Picking it up recently, I recalled only a rough outline: an Irish Catholic boy's coming of age amid strife in Northern Ireland. And I remembered that it had haunted me. I finished reading it on the night of January 6, 2021, hours after United States citizens stormed the Capitol in protest of the presidential election results. Appalling images of the frenzied mob filled our screens. I felt overwhelmed by shock, anger, and sorrow. A few times that night, I turned away from the TV, picked up my book, and slipped into the besieged territory of another time and place.

In *Reading in the Dark*, the unnamed narrator tells of growing up in Derry, Northern Ireland, his childhood marred by the history and present-day of the Troubles. Spanning 1945-1961, with a brief final scene set in 1971, the novel contains chapters comprised of vignettes whose titles create a disturbing narrative of their own:

"Accident," "Pistol," "Fire," "Blood," "The Feud," "Field of the Disappeared," and so on. Ghosts haunt the narrator's home—or so his mother seems to believe. An old slaughterhouse and the ruins of a whiskey distillery blown up by the British provide the backdrop for his and his friends' neighborhood wanderings. Secrets fester, for men on both sides of the family have a long history with the Irish Republican Army. When the narrator at around eight years of age throws a rock at a police car to distract a bully about to assault him, the repercussions are far more grievous than he had ever anticipated.

The narrator leavens such grimness by describing excursions into the countryside—with its sea air and the cry of gulls, its caves and rock formations from time immemorial, its folklore and folk heroes. As always, however, human conflict implicates the landscape, as in a vignette called "Grianan"—the Giant's Causeway, "a great stone ring with flights of worn steps on the inside leading to a parapet that overlooked the countryside in one direction and the coastal sands of the lough in the other." Inside was a "wishing chair of slabbed stone. You sat there and closed your eyes and wished for what you wanted most, while you listened for the breathing of the sleeping warriors of the legendary Fianna who lay below," the narrator says.

One hot summer afternoon, on a rare holiday, the narrator's father takes him and his brother Liam to an outcropping known as the Field of the Disappeared, where "the souls of all those from the area who had disappeared or had never had a Christian burial. . . collected three or four times a year . . . to cry like birds and look down on the fields where they had been born. Any human who entered the field would suffer the same fate; and any who heard their cries on those days should cross themselves and pray out loud to drown out the sound." The narrator wonders whether this was where the restless soul of his Uncle Eddie, his father's brother, came to mourn his lost patrimony. Although he doesn't ask, he senses much more that his father isn't telling him. Years later, he realizes his father had been trying to convey to him the location's significance in the chain of events concerning Eddie's demise.

*****

Before I knew better, which took an embarrassingly long time, I viewed Ireland in the superficial light of a picture postcard. I imagined green fields, rocky shores, fluffy sheep, and beautiful woolens. Ireland possesses all these things, but I was wholly ignorant of the reality on the ground. When I was a child, my awareness of Ireland began and ended with Mary Mast, née Faul, my mother's best friend and a second mother to me, who lived across the street. Our two families had children about the same ages, and we all grew up together. Mary was from Louth Village, about an hour north of Dublin by the coast and several miles south of the border with Northern Ireland. Cecilia (Cece) and her twin, Brian, were the same age as my brother, three years older than I, but she and I were close friends, throughout grade school especially.

I remember the packages her mother's sisters, Auntie Bid and Auntie Eleanor, would send from Ireland, full of comic books, candies, and Lucky Bags: treats wrapped in newspaper and colored tissue. I especially loved the Smarties, equivalent to our M&Ms. I remember when the aunts would visit and stay for a few weeks, times when the Mast house rang with laughter and Irish accents, enchanting to my ears. And I remember my mother telling me about a time she was over at Mary's when her sisters were visiting, the four of them talking, laughing, and, in a sign of the times, smoking cigarettes late into the night. At some point, my mother mentioned "Londonderry," and the three Faul women became incensed. "It's *Derry!*" they exclaimed as my mother sheepishly apologized. This was my introduction to Irish political fervor. That and watching the video of U2's live performance of "Sunday Bloody Sunday" hundreds of times on MTV.

The song's title referred to the day Irish civilians had been killed by British police. Like millions of other young people at the time, I found the video enthralling: the song's powerful drumbeat, Bono's strutting around the stage, the crowd's roars and cheers. "Sunday Bloody Sunday" came across as a principled stand against injustice—but at thirteen years old, I didn't know what exactly the principle, stand, or injustice were. As Harry Browne writes in his book on Bono, "Bloody Sunday can refer to two events in Irish history: a date during the War of Independence of 1920 when the IRA killed British intelligence officers across Dublin, and soldiers retaliated by shooting into a Gaelic-football crowd in Croke Parke, killing fourteen spectators; or an afternoon in 1972 when British paratroopers again killed fourteen unarmed civilians, this time after a civil rights march in Derry, Northern Ireland."

With Ireland on my mind, I sent Cece a message mentioning the (London) Derry story and that *Reading in the Dark* had prompted the memory. She wrote back about her uncle, Denis Faul, a priest and prominent civil rights activist who was instrumental in ending the 1981 hunger strikes undertaken by Irish political prisoners. "Because my Uncle Denis was so embroiled in the Troubles up north," Cece wrote, "we were not permitted to discuss it nor were we encouraged to read about it." He was a controversial figure, "as outspoken against the IRA as he was the British," she said. I Googled his name and learned that in addition to his role in ending the hunger strikes, he also "campaigned for the release of the Birmingham Six and the Guildford Four and the McGuire Seven before their causes became well-known and vindicated." He co-authored numerous books, such as *H Blocks: British Jail for Irish Political Prisoners* and *The Hooded Men: British Torture in Ireland, August, October 1971*. "He stared down the barrel of many a British and IRA rifle," Cece wrote.

I was fascinated by his story. I remembered meeting him once when he was visiting Mary and her family. I told my mother afterward that he didn't look me in the eye when we were introduced and that I found that strange. "I'm not surprised," she said. "Priests rarely deign to look girls or women in the eye," a comment rooted in her many years of feminist activism. Cece added *Reading in the Dark* to her reading list, and I asked if she had read *Say Nothing: A True Story of Murder and Memory in Northern Ireland*, by Patrick Radden Keefe, which I knew of through book reviews but hadn't yet read. She said it was on her nightstand and that she remembers as a child hearing about the kidnapping of widowed mother of ten, Jean McConville, the event at the center of *Say Nothing* from which Keefe's history of the Troubles unspools.

*****

In the 1980s, when I was in high school, rumors circulated that Notre Dame professors were funneling money and arms to the IRA.

Where would I have heard such a thing? And which professors? Ours was a Notre Dame neighborhood, the campus less than a mile away. Most of the families up and down the street and for blocks in every direction had one or both parents on the faculty. I never asked about these rumors, spoken in hushed, anxious voices—but I could have. A political science professor, my father would have welcomed such questions, but I wouldn't have known how to begin. I had no frame of reference, although I vividly recall watching my father watch a story on the news one night about the Troubles. He stood in front of the television with a frown on his face. For people like Mary Mast, the fear was palpable. "My mom was terrified through most of the '70s and '80s," Cece wrote, "so, in typical Irish fashion, she repressed it."

Cece also told me that the title *Say Nothing* comes from Seamus Heaney's poem "Whatever You Say, Say Nothing"—and Heaney's title quotes a poster that appeared in Northern Ireland during the Troubles showing an armed, uniformed IRA paramilitary in a balaclava and bearing a message comprised of collaged bits of magazine and newspaper print: "Loose-lips cost lives In taxis On the phone In clubs and bars At football matches At home with friends Anywhere Whatever you say—say nothing." Paramilitaries deployed the injunction to "say nothing" as a threat, a means of instilling fear and enforcing silence in their ranks. They meted out fierce discipline to those suspected of "loose lips." In April 2016, the *Irish News* reported that the posters had reappeared on the International Wall in west Belfast. The news story also mentions Heaney's four-part poem.

*****

"Whatever You Say, Say Nothing" begins with the speaker "writing just after an encounter / With an English journalist in search of 'views / On the Irish thing'"—the word "thing" characteristic of the press's downplaying of the strife and dehumanization of the Irish. The "jottings and analyses" of the "media-men" are rife with bias and clichés and serve only to exacerbate the discord and violence, the speaker states. He calls out English politicians and journalists for disregarding Irish suffering and for demanding the internment of IRA activists despite the atrocities perpetrated by the British and the unionists. The betrayals and blasted landscapes of Northern Ireland rise up in Heaney's poem like a hydra. "This morning from a dewy motorway / I saw the new camp for the internees," the speaker states. "A bomb had left a crater of fresh clay / In the roadside, and over in the trees / Machine-gun posts defined a real stockade."

While the entire poem resonates with *Reading in the Dark*, Part III most strongly evokes the experiences of the novel's narrator. "'Religion's never mentioned here,' of course," the section begins, evoking the hypocrisies, prejudices, and double-talk of factions in the North. "'You know them by their eyes,' and hold your tongue. / 'One side's bad as the other,' never worse"—this last comment a supposedly neutral one that disgusts the poem's speaker: "Christ, it's near time that some small leak was sprung / In the great dykes the Dutchman made / To dam the dangerous tide that followed Seamus." Further harming the Irish living in the North is the unwritten rule among them that "to be saved you only must save face / And whatever you say, you say nothing." Children were warned never to divulge information about themselves lest they be pegged as Catholic, or Protestant, and harmed. "Smoke-signals are loud-mouthed compared with us," Heaney writes. Yet by remaining silent, the Irish become complicit in their own oppression in a "land of password, handgrip, wink and nod, / Of open minds as open as a trap, / Where tongues lie coiled, as under flames lie wicks, / Where half of us, as in a wooden horse / Were cabin'd and confined like wily Greeks, / Besieged within the siege, whispering morse."

The directive to say nothing permeates *Reading in the Dark*. The narrator relates the many conversations he overheard throughout the years between his father and uncles about what happened in the 1920s—to Uncle Eddie and to Aunt Katie's husband in particular. Nothing is certain, however, as aspects of the story alternately coalesce or clash with each other. Family lore carries the ring of truth, but the chaos of one night in particular, along with his parents' repression of the trauma, places key details forever out of reach. "A choice, an election, was to be made," the narrator decides, "between what actually happened and what I imagined, what I had heard, what I kept hearing" about the night his father's older brother, Eddie, met his fate. Details are jumbled. "Maybe I had imagined and should try to forget it," he says of "a story about one of the IRA men in the distillery strapping himself to an upright iron girder at the corner of the building as it caught fire."

Similar uncertainty involves the gun Eddie carried that night—"a First World War rifle that had belonged to a Black-and-Tan soldier killed in the War of Independence . . . Was it Dan who had said this? Or Katie? Or Grandfather? I didn't know. I could hear all their voices in the kitchen but I couldn't match a voice to a detail. . . . Much of it must have been ornament, people making strange little alliances in their heads between things they had heard or read about, seeking to assert themselves in those endless conversations, implying they were in the know, there was much else they could tell, but . . .," he trails off. Such is the subjective, piecemeal nature of memory.

His grandfather's deathbed confession to his daughter (the narrator's mother) only worsens the trauma. As the narrator gradually pieces together the truth, he imagines a conversation he might have with his mother in which they both divulge their long-held secrets. He despairs of any such resolution, however, for there remain too many unknowns. "And how did I know I had been told the truth?" he wonders. "Shouldn't I just ask her? What did you know, Mother, when you married my father? Why did you silence me, over and over?" Ultimately, he too chooses silence in the hopes of protecting his mother and especially his father even though it means driving a wedge between them. "Staying loyal to my mother made me disloyal to my father," he says. "In case I should ever be tempted to tell him all I knew, I stayed at arm's length from him and saw him notice but could say nothing to explain." Yet in contemplating his father deeply, he develops profound compassion for him—perhaps more so than if there had been no secrets at all.

*****

Reading in the Dark makes for an intense reading experience that prompted a constellation of memories and reflections. Because of this novel, I reached out to one of my oldest and dearest friends, evoking those long-ago years when our families were so deeply interlaced. Cece's revelations of the Troubles' presence in her childhood home provided insights into her family and the resilience of parents who shield their children from the harshest of life's realities. I have a new stack of books to read on Irish history and the Troubles, a new collection of Heaney poems, and a further means of bonding with a close friend who's an expert in, and passionate about, Irish literature. I also think of the pull Ireland continues to exert on people I love.

My oldest niece minored in Irish literature and language at Notre Dame. She spent a week in Dublin and two weeks in a remote part of Connemara between her sophomore and junior years and four weeks the following summer in Glencolumbkille, a tiny town in county Donegal. Her first summer there, during a stopover in Galway, she and a friend went for a walk and happened upon the writer Colm Tóibín sitting on a bench eating his lunch. He was due to give a talk in Galway later that day, which my niece and the other students had plans to attend. They exchanged hellos and wound up chatting. My niece had Tóibín's novel *Brooklyn* in her bag—she had recognized him from the author photo on the back—and he signed it for her. After a few minutes, the woman who was with him, in some professional capacity, whisked him away. I was already a Tóibín fan, but when I learned about this happy encounter, I thought, this man was kind to my niece? I will buy everything he's ever written.

My husband and I travelled to Dublin for a few days in March 2001. We hopped over from London, where we were staying with my parents for a couple of weeks while my father was head of Notre Dame's London program for the semester. We happened to land in Dublin on St. Patrick's Day, and during our short visit, we enjoyed touring the city, including paying homage at Joyce-related monuments and sites. We went to the Dublin Writers Museum, the Guinness Brewery, to Trinity College to see the Book of Kells, and for drinks at the Brazen Head, Ireland's oldest pub. And I bought beautiful woolens. Any trip outside the city was off-limits as the U.K. was experiencing an outbreak of foot-and-mouth disease, and every effort was made to keep it from spreading.

Back in London, my husband and I would go sightseeing all day and regroup at my parents' apartment before heading back out at night. We'd unwind while watching *The Weakest Link*. And we watched horrific scenes on the news of towering piles of burning carcasses—livestock that had been killed by the millions to stop the spread of foot-and-mouth. There were also reports of farmers who had died by suicide, in despair at having lost everything. It's with misgivings, then, that I look back on our trip as wonderful overall. But for us, it was—not least because my parents were healthy at the time. The years of walkers and wheelchairs, cancers and surgeries lay far ahead. My mother made it over to Ireland that semester, too, to visit the Fauls. I enjoy picturing her with them, talking and laughing, going on excursions, and tracing her own Irish genealogy. While it may be too soon after my parents' deaths to reflect as intently on their marriage and inner lives as the narrator of *Reading in the Dark* does with his parents, I can see faint outlines bearing their shapes in the distance ahead—or perhaps it's the distance behind—that I will strive to shade in as time passes.

Chapter 4

Luka and the Fire of Life
by Salman Rushdie

Merry Christmas, 2010
Kristin from
Mom and Dad – love

I don't know that my parents ever read Salman Rushdie. I don't remember seeing any of his books in our house when I was growing up or in later years. I imagine my mother chose *Luka and the Fire of Life* because several years previously, I had talked about teaching Rushdie and attending a talk of his. Or maybe she was drawn to Niroot Puttapitat's gorgeous and evocative cover illustration: two lithe figures in silhouette seated on a luminous flying carpet. In any event, the book stood patiently on a shelf amid a few other Rushdie novels for eleven years before I reached for it in the spring of 2021. I didn't know the first thing about it. I hadn't read any reviews or come across the title in my online book browsing, and to my knowledge, no one I knew had read it, either. The cover exerted a pull, however, perhaps as it had on my mother before me, and I picked it up, ready for whatever might lie within.

As Woolf's Clarissa Dalloway might say, what a lark, what a plunge it was to be swept into the thrilling world of *Luka and the Fire of Life*! The story opens upon 12-year-old Luka Khalifa nestled in a loving home with his mother, Soraya, his professional storyteller father, Rashid (the Ocean of Notions to his admirers, the Shah of Blah to his detractors), his 18-years-older brother, Haroun, and his two pets: Dog, the bear, and Bear, the dog. I realized the novel was a sequel as a few pages in, Haroun says to Luka, "You've reached the age at which people in this family cross the border into the magical world. It's your turn for an adventure—yes, it's finally here!—and it certainly looks like you've started something now," for Luka has recently cursed an evil circus manager, Captain Aag, who had been harming his animals. "May your animals stop obeying your commands and your rings of fire eat up your stupid tent," Luka had shouted. Soon, Aag's animals stage a mutiny and walk out on him, ruining his lucrative business. Next, Dog, the bear, and Bear, the dog, show up at Luka's door. "*An adventure of my very own*, Luka thought in wonderment . . . When Haroun had been Luka's age he had traveled to the Earth's second moon, befriended fishes who spoke in rhyme and a gardener made of lotus roots, and helped to overthrow the evil Cultmaster Khattam-Shud, who was trying to destroy the Sea of Stories itself." Rushdie wrote *Haroun and the Sea of Stories* in 1990 at the request of his young son, Zafar, who "kept badgering me to write a book that he could read," Rushdie explained in an interview. It was also his first novel after *The Satanic Verses* and the first since Ayatollah Ruhollah Khomeini issued the fatwa in 1989 calling for Rushdie's death. Two decades later, Rushdie's young son, Milan, wanted his own special story—thus *Luka and the Fire of Life*. I wondered if I should read *Haroun* first but forged ahead with *Luka*, for after just a few pages, I was hooked.

*****

Rashid Khalifa is a good-natured man who spins intricate, interconnected stories for the bright, curious son sitting on his lap or lying in his bed preparing for sleep. Tickling plays a major role in their relationship, too. When Rashid's health begins to decline for no discernable reason, the family grows concerned. "He walked more slowly than before (though he had never walked quickly), ate more slowly (though not very much more), and, most worrying of all, talked more slowly (and he had always talked very, very fast)." When he sinks into a deep sleep lasting for days, then weeks, Haroun, Soraya, and Luka become frantic—Luka especially so, for he has reason to believe that whatever ails his father is all his fault. One night, he had looked out his bedroom window and seen seven vultures circling:

They were ugly, smelly, and mean. The biggest, ugliest, smelliest, and meanest vulture settled down on Luka's windowsill, right next to him, as if they were old friends, while the other six hovered out of reach. . . . Hanging from the ruff around the Boss Vulture's neck was a little pouch. . . . Inside the pouch was a scroll of paper, and on the scroll of paper was a message from Captain Aag: "Dreadful black-tongued child," the message read. "Disgusting witch-boy, did you imagine I would do nothing in return for what you did to me? . . . Throw out a curse when you can't control it, O incompetent pygmy hexer, and it will come back to smack you in the face. Or, on this occasion, in perhaps an even more satisfying act of revenge, it poleaxes someone you love."

The next morning, Luka sees his father standing outside in the lane—which makes no sense, because his father also lies asleep down the hall. Rushing outside, Luka finds that the man in the street is a shade of sorts, a semi see-through presence who looks, talks, and dresses like Rashid and has come to await Rashid's death. "As his father faded away," Luka realizes, "the phantom Rashid would grow stronger, and in the end there would be only this Nobodaddy and no father at all. But he was very sure of one thing: he was not ready to do without a father. . . . There was only one thing for it, he told himself. This, this Nobodaddy had to be stopped, and he had to think of a way to stop him." Thus begins Luka's great adventure in the World of Magic, a beguiling parallel realm harboring the carefully guarded Fire of Life, "which burned in the Mountain of Knowledge, which stood by the Lake of Wisdom, which was illuminated by the Dawn of Days." It has the power, Nobodaddy tells Luka, to save his father's life.

Absconding with the Fire of Life will be no small feat, however. In the World of Magic, Luka, along with Bear, the dog, and Dog, the bear, meets with myriad adventures and fantastical creatures, both friend and foe. To capture the Fire of Life, they must pass a series of challenges, accumulating or losing lives by the hundreds, logged in a tiny digital counter perceptible to Luka out of the corner of his eye. His obsession with video games, which his father had always encouraged and which his mother had scorned as a waste of time, serves him well. He swoops, swerves, and dodges obstacles, sometimes physically and sometimes by his wits—or he enlists creatures from the World of Magic who can finagle safe passage for him. Aspects of this world frighten and confuse Luka, but at the same time, he finds it all reassuringly familiar, for it is his father's invention, and he's been hearing about it all his life. "The Magical World, once kept hidden and guarded, had been made available to the general public by Rashid Khalifa in many celebrated tales."

I was thrilled to accompany Luka and his friends on their adventure, especially on their principal mode of transportation: Resham the flying carpet. I cruised along with them at breakneck speed, away from a harrowing pandemic year that wreaked havoc all over the world. My husband and I were extraordinarily fortunate through it all. We kept our jobs and worked from home in comfort and security. We didn't catch Covid (that would come later), and no one in our immediate families did, either. Several close friends suffered terrible losses from Covid-19, though, losing a father, a mother-in-law, a 28-year-old brother. We mourned the dead—590 thousand in the United States and three and a half million worldwide as I write this in May 2021. As winter turned into spring, the tide turned a bit. Covid rates began creeping down, and more and more people were getting vaccinated, including ourselves. After 14 months, we could finally travel and visit my husband's 91-year-old mother. Social distancing restrictions were gradually lifting as well. Reading *Luka and the Fire of Life* came as a welcome relief from the horrors around us. And thinking of Rushdie revived memories of another notable period in our lives.

*****

In the mid-1990s, I began tracking Booker Prize-winning novels, which led me to Rushdie's *Midnight's Children*, winner of the Booker in 1981 (and chosen in 2011 as the greatest Booker Prize-winning novel of all-time: the Booker of Bookers). I found *Midnight's Children* wondrous, a tour de force the likes of which I had never encountered before. Not long after reading it, I was hired as a visiting assistant professor of English at the University of Louisville, and one of my courses that first semester, Fall 2005, was Colonial and

Postcolonial Literature. I put *Midnight's Children* on my syllabus, and my class spent two weeks reading and discussing it.

As it happened, Rushdie gave a lecture at Bellarmine University in Louisville later that semester. My class of eight and I went together—that is, when I walked into the auditorium and looked for them, I saw hands waving and beckoning to me. My students were already there and had saved me a seat. A newly minted Ph.D. with a major case of impostor syndrome, I was flattered and touched by their welcoming me into their group. The event was called "Step Across This Line: An Evening of Salman Rushdie," and I confess I don't really remember what he said. I know he spoke about the importance of storytelling and the global, shared nature of stories. What I do remember is being utterly mesmerized by him. He was gracious and brilliant, and I could have listened to his melodious voice all night. He had just published *Shalimar the Clown*, and I stood in line to buy a copy and have him sign it along with my well-worn copy of *Midnight's Children*.

*****

I loved teaching at Louisville. I had finished my Ph.D. just a year before and was eager, energetic, and overjoyed at having landed a full-time job, if not tenure-track. I had wonderful colleagues and was fortunate to share an office that year with the writer Sena Jeter Naslund. I knew I had heard or read her name before but couldn't quite place it. Looking around the office during my first week, I noticed that the bookshelves held multiple copies, in different languages, of the novel *Ahab's Wife*. I put two and two together and realized I was sharing an office with a famous author. We weren't often in there at the same time, but when we were, we chatted amicably, and she was lovely to me. After I read *Ahab's Wife*, she asked if I would like to go for a coffee and talk about it, ask any questions I might have. Along with Rushdie's lecture, listening to Sena discuss her breakout novel and her writing process was a highlight of that year.

I couldn't spend much time socializing, however, because I was living in Cincinnati and commuting to Louisville—two hours each way, two or three times a week. I would drive down, teach four 75-minute classes, hold office hours, and drive home. I left the house between 6:30 and 7:00 in the morning and arrived home around 10:00 at night. I still can't believe I did it for two years—and I'm still thankful I never hit a deer. The highway shoulders were littered with their poor carcasses, especially in the fall. The drive was uneventful most days, but there were also a number of traffic jams and construction delays. Once, there was a terrible truck accident that I later learned had killed two people. Driving by at the time, I saw enormous blue tarps covering a swath of ground in the median. From that day forward, driving by that spot, I didn't pray, exactly, but I thought of the two souls who lost their lives that day and wished them well on their journey. It made me less apt to complain of my own exhausting routine, especially knowing how extraordinarily fortunate I was to have a job at all given the atrocious state of the academic job market, especially in English. I was still on the market as Louisville's policy, like that of so many other universities, was not to hire their visiting assistant professors into the tenure-track. I've never understood that policy, and I thought it a shame. I loved teaching there, and my course evaluations from those two years were the best I ever received.

Like thousands of others, so alarmingly similar, I trudged off to interview for jobs at the Modern Language Association convention that winter, in Washington, D.C. The following spring, within a three-week span, I travelled out of town four times: twice to present papers at conferences and twice for on-campus job interviews. I presented a paper a third time at Louisville's own literary conference—all while prepping classes, teaching, grading, and commuting. When my last class ended at 7:45 p.m. the Thursday before spring break began, after the last student walked out of the room, I burst into tears. I cried walking to the parking lot and getting into my car. I cried all the way home—and it poured that night, the rain and my tears forming a double layer of streaming water to peer through while driving two hours in the dark. I cried unlocking our front door. I cried quietly while getting ready for bed so as not to wake my husband—all for naught because I cried when I got into bed and woke him up anyway. The pent-up exhaustion, stress, and tension—of the crazy routine, the commute, the traveling, and above all the soul-destroying experience that is the academic job market—had burst through and could not be stoppered.

I was hired on for a second year at Louisville. I enjoyed my classes and students, and I survived the long days and job market stress. In Fall 2006, I taught *Maus Volume 1: My Father Bleeds History* in my Literary Theory and Criticism class, a capstone course for English majors, and got to meet Art Spiegelman when he visited campus to talk and give a reading. I was also involved in planning a campus visit and reading by the author Gish Jen. It was a wonderful two years, and my job market story ended happily, for I wound up back at Georgetown College, where I had been in 2004-2005 as a visiting assistant professor, and eventually on the tenure-track there. My memories of my time at the University of Louisville remain vivid and will always be intertwined with Salman Rushdie, no matter how much time goes by.

In fact, it is its handling of time that I find most intriguing about *Luka and the Fire of Life*, for Luka's journey carries him up the River of Time, in which "the whole history of everything was flowing along before his very eyes, transformed into shining, mingling, multicolored story streams." He must also pass through the Mists of Time, the Limits of Memory, and Oblivion, which prompt philosophical musings to which we can all surely relate. "If Time was a River, eternally flowing," Luka wonders:

> did that mean that the Past would always be there and the Future, too, already existed? . . . But on the other hand, if Time flowed like a River then surely the Past would have flowed away already, in which case how could he go back into it to find the Fire of Life . . . ? And if the Past had flowed away, then what was back there at the River's source? And if the future already existed, then perhaps it didn't matter what he, Luka, did next, because no matter how hard he was trying to save his father's life, maybe Rashid Khalifa's fate had already been decided.

Learning that the Past, Present, and Future—the Aalim—stand guard over the Fire of Life prompts further reflections on the vagaries of time.

*****

Like Luka, I struggle with the nature of time, especially since my parents died. I of course understand that everyone must die. That my parents had good long lives and that it was time for them to go. That I would not have wanted them to linger and suffer, shells of their former selves in bodies and minds that had betrayed them. But I don't know how to be at peace with such concepts. I don't understand how it's possible that my parents are gone or that my brother, sister, and I are in our fifties. That I'm developing arthritis in my hands. That my childhood friends have knee replacements and mastectomy scars. When I listen to music from the '80s, it takes my breath away—not because I want to go back to that time but because time passes so inconceivably fast. When Luka strives to slow down time so he can reach the Fire of Life and save his dying father, I'm cheering him on, wishing that a magical being, or a determined and clever 12-year-old like him, had swooped in to restore my parents' health, too.

It was an affliction of Rashid's that had set his older son's adventure into motion as well. Early in *Haroun and the Sea of Stories*, Soraya, feeling neglected, leaves Rashid for another man, whereupon he loses his gift for storytelling. I'm a bit annoyed that Rushdie dredged up the tired old canard of a woman's betrayal to propel his narrative, especially since Rashid was, in fact, neglecting his wife, devoting all his time and energy to storytelling. Soraya is a bit of a killjoy in *Luka* as well. "In spite of a life spent with the fabled Shah of Blah, Soraya Khalifa had never entirely liked this fanciful stuff, which she now had to put up with from both her sons as well as her storyteller husband." Far more disturbing, however, is the silencing of a brilliant storyteller—Rushdie's experience of the fatwa. He would continue to champion literary freedom and freedom of expression around the world, but in *Haroun and the Sea of Stories*, as Rashid stands before a street crowd, on a stage, or at a podium, all that comes out of his mouth is a strange, dry croak. Not only is his livelihood at stake but also stories and storytelling themselves, essential to our survival as a species. After entering the magical realm, Haroun learns that a dictator and his minions have terrorized the people into silence. They are also deliberately poisoning the Sea of Stories, for they know the people will become unthinking and more obedient in a world devoid of imagination.

When Luka finally confronts the Aalim, they speak "in unison . . . 'Compassion is not our affair,'" they declare. "'The ages go by heartlessly whether people wish them to do so or not. All things must pass. . . . Happiness, friendship, love, suffering, pain are fleeting illusions, like shadows on a wall. The seconds march forward into minutes, the minutes into days, the days into years, unfeelingly. . . . Only this knowledge is Wisdom. This wisdom alone is Knowledge.'" In my darker moments, I'm inclined to believe them as I contemplate the years having slipped through my fingers like the shimmery, liquid story strands coursing up the River of Time. I don't want to live in the past or with regrets, but with each passing day, I'm increasingly aware of all that I took for granted—although as a character in Rachel Cusk's *Outline* says, the cruel trick is that we can't possibly realize what we took for granted until it's gone. I guess I thought my parents would be around forever, that I could decline my mother's offer of a glass of wine or my father's invitation to drive over to look at the new buildings going up on Notre Dame's campus. That there would always be time. Out for a walk one recent morning, I burst into tears and apologized to my father for being such a shit sometimes.

Luka would have no patience with such wallowing, for he stands undeterred by the Aalim's grim pronouncement.

"Then I curse you, just as I cursed Captain Aag!" he yelled . . . "You think you have everyone in your cage, and so you can ignore us and torment us and make us do what you want, and you don't care about anything except yourselves. Well, curse you, all three of you! What are you, anyway? . . . The only sure thing is that we—Bear, Dog, my family, my friends, and us—*we* will make it whatever it is, good or bad, happy or sad, and we certainly don't need you to tell us what it is. Time isn't a trap, you phoneys. It's just the road I'm on, and I'm in a real hurry right now, so get out of my way . . ." So there it was. He had defied Time's power, just as his mother (and, later, his father) had said he could.

I think I should create a broadside out of this speech.

As the novel draws to a close, Luka briefly wonders "how it would be if his brother, his mother, and his father could all live forever. The idea struck him as more frightening than exciting. Maybe his dog, Bear, had been right, and it was better to do without Immortality, or even the possibility of it." He realizes he needs to put his adventure behind him, "and the Real world would be Real again, and life would be just that, life, and that would be more than enough." The family continues eating, talking, and laughing. And Soraya? She gets everybody up and dancing on the rooftop under the stars.

*****

Postscript: On August 12, 2022, as he prepared to give a talk at the Chautauqua Institution in Chautauqua, New York, Salman Rushdie was attacked and stabbed multiple times by a man presumably trying to carry out the fatwa. For weeks, he lay in a hospital recovering from grievous injuries, including a damaged liver and severed nerves in his arm. He also lost sight in one eye. I thought of him a great deal during this time—his brilliance, his bravery, his defense of free speech—and I shed tears for his suffering. On August 19, a week after the attack, a crowd gathered on the steps of the New York Public Library in support of Salman Rushdie. They read aloud from his works, including *The Satanic Verses*, and lauded his commitment to literary freedom. I joined others around the globe in wishing him well. Six months later, he began talking about the attack and promoting the novel he had finished just before it happened, *Victory City*.

Chapter 5

Mrs. Woolf and the Servants: An Intimate History of Domestic Life in Bloomsbury

by Alison Light

9/22/2008
Dear Kristin,
Congratulations on your 38th [sic]
birthday.
I hope you enjoy this book
about an insufferable snob.
Love,
Mom

I knew Virginia Woolf's name long before I read her as her books were scattered around our house when I grew up—worn paperbacks of *Jacob's Room, Mrs. Dalloway, To the Lighthouse, A Room of One's Own*, and *Three Guineas* along with the six-volume paperback set of the letters. A few of the books had my sister's signature inside. I don't know whether she read them for school or on her own. Little did I realize when eyeing these books in the floor-to-ceiling bookcases in the dining room of my childhood home how momentous a role Woolf would come to play in my life. My mother reread *A Room of One's Own* late in her own life, and when she finished, she called to talk with me about how brilliant and revolutionary the book remains to this day. Given her lifelong Anglophilia and my own investment in all things Woolf, I know my mother was excited to give me Alison Light's *Mrs. Woolf and the Servants*, a fascinating work of history, biography, cultural critique, and literary criticism. In pulling back the curtain on the upstairs/downstairs worlds of English homes over the centuries, the book was a joy for my mother to read. She was eager for me to read it, too, so we could dish about it together.

Over the years, Bloomsbury-bashing readers and academics have delighted in cherry-picking quotations from Woolf's letters and diaries that expose her in the most unflattering light, such as her snarky remarks about servants—her own, her sister's, and servants in general as an essential but amorphous (to her) group in English society. Unfortunately, there are many such quotations to choose from, and they butt up against a countervailing image of Woolf as iconoclast. As Light notes in her preface, "Virginia's dependence on her servants plays havoc with any easy celebration of either her or her sister, the painter Vanessa Bell, as bohemian, free women, creating a new kind of life." Vanessa especially maintained the slightly haughty demeanor of the Victorian mistress when doling out her servants' instructions each morning. Yet "servants don't usually feature in accounts of 'Bloomsbury's women,'" Light states. "Idealizing visions of [Bloomsbury's women] as heroines often go hand in hand with a romantic view of art which imagines it to be the product of lonely genius. But without all the domestic care and hard work which servants provided there would have been no art, no writing, no 'Bloomsbury.'"

While Virginia and Vanessa eagerly shook off the dusty remnants of their Victorian upbringing, they never relinquished the expectation that women of their social class must keep servants. Vanessa, for instance, "often found servants 'tiresome,'" writes Light, but "she believed she had little option. No one of her generation and class looked after their own children even if they didn't want to paint." For Virginia, who craved uninterrupted stretches of time to read and write, contending with live-in servants became a source of frustration, humiliation, and anxiety. Her complaints about them were legion, although as Light explains, they, along with other "offensive passages in Virginia's writing about the poor or the suburban, about 'the Jew' or 'negroes,' can be matched by others equally vile in the work of many of her contemporaries. But she was highly unusual in examining many of her reactions and feelings, probing her sore spots, especially in her diaries." In her fiction, she continually sought to capture the lives of the lower classes—the shop girl, the lavatory attendant, the obscure—all of whom she believed just as worthy of literary representation as the society hostess, the war veteran, the philosopher, or the late-Victorian matriarch.

Nevertheless, members of the Bloomsbury Group imbued their servant situations with intrigue and drama. Light writes of the "innumerable passages about the servants in the diaries and letters of Virginia Woolf, her husband and their circle; so many, in fact, that editors have been embarrassed by their superfluity—at one point in the 1910s, Virginia and … Vanessa … write every day about their servants' doings." At the same time,

> there is a long history of not noticing or valuing servants, seeing them as functionaries or mere types. It rankled with many servants at the time and continues to annoy some of their descendants, as I was to discover. Percy Bartholomew, for instance, was Leonard Woolf's gardener for twenty-odd years, but Leonard discusses his character in his autobiography without once giving his surname. Percy's son, Jim, remained furious about this.

Light also notes Leonard's "insistence in his autobiography that [he and Virginia] were 'servantless'" by the 1930s "while employing both Percy and Louie," their day maid.

The women in service in Bloomsbury flats, at Vanessa's home, Charleston, and at Virginia and Leonard's Rodmell home, Monk's House, toiled hard for low wages and in subpar living conditions—a cramped room off the kitchen with no privacy or an attic that was stifling in summer and freezing in winter. Daily tasks for servants in any such household at the time included shopping for food and cooking the meals, changing and making the beds, scrubbing the floors and flues, and contending with the endless work of the scullery in dark, dank basements. Most contentious of all, it seems, was the emptying of chamber pots and sewage—"a serious issue among the servants since it affected their earnings and their self-respect." While contemporary photographs of Monk's House give off a serene minimalist vibe, it was far different when Virginia and Leonard lived there. "Monk's House remained messy, dusty and smelly," Light writes, "and their marmoset, Mitzi, had erratic bladder control; there were platters on the floor for the cats and dogs, piles of books, ashtrays and general clutter, and open fires," all of which made housekeeping challenging for their servants. Light's extensive archival work and empathy invest all the servants she discusses with unique personalities and complex lives of their own. Romances, families, ambitions, likes and dislikes—they were there all along yet often overlooked or disregarded by their employers, not to mention by historians of England and the Bloomsbury Group.

All told, however, servants at Charleston and Monk's House had it better than many others. "In the first place, there was no uniform," Light explains:

> Nor were you called by your surname . . . Virginia and Vanessa were 'Mrs Woolf' and 'Mrs Bell' and not the customary 'Ma'am.' . . . These were very informal households. No one dressed for dinner . . . there was no waiting at meals. . . . Other fetching and carrying was at a minimum. Neither Mrs Woolf nor Mrs Bell supervised their servants while they worked, and to most of their class their manners would have appeared unbelievably lax.

In sum, "Bloomsbury was sociable and fun . . . There were many parties, including fancy dress, to which the servants were often invited . . . Monk's House rang with laughter" due to the maid, Lottie's, shenanigans and pranks, such as dropping a marzipan mouse into Virginia's tea. "No doubt the servants had good times in Bloomsbury," Light concludes.

*****

It's hard for me to imagine a world in which live-in servants are the norm. I suppose the closest thing I ever experienced in my own life were the cleaning women employed by some of my friends' parents when I was growing up. My brother, sister, and I went to an expensive private grade school, and to my eyes, many of my classmates were "rich"—in quotation marks because I don't know what would have constituted "rich" in those days, nor did I have any idea how much money anyone's parents made, including my own. But I had friends with bigger, fancier homes, in-ground swimming pools, and Mercedes and BMWs in the garage (we had a Toyota Corona) along with more—and more expensive—clothing and toys. Most of these families had cleaning women. Or housekeepers. Or maids. I'm not sure how they were referred to. My friend Judy's family had an African American cleaning woman named Hazel. I remember her working in their house on Friday afternoons. Our grade school let out at 11:35 a.m. on Fridays, and I often went to Judy's house for the rest of the day or to stay overnight. I remember Hazel moving about in a dress and apron. I remember a few of us acting up one day, being loud and obnoxious. I can still see Hazel looking down at us from the top of the stairs. Even then I felt abashed and wondered what on earth she must have thought of us.

The family of another friend who lived just a few blocks away had a housekeeper, too, a Polish woman named Stella, whom I encountered from time to time. I suppose she came once a week or maybe every two weeks. She seemed quite old and like she had difficulty getting around. She moved very slowly, bent over, the way my mother would eventually walk due to painful spinal stenosis. At my friend's house, we would say hello to Stella and then make ourselves scarce. Did we do so to let her clean in peace? Or because we were embarrassed? Or because she seemed from another world, and we didn't know how to act around her? Other friends' families had cleaning women, too. Their houses were always spotless. I didn't necessarily envy this, but I did note that things were different in my house, where the living room was always neat as a pin but where other rooms showed the disorder that comes from a family of five going about their lives. As I got a bit older, I grew more self-conscious. These friends spent the night at my house, too. On a few occasions, I asked my mother if she could please tidy up the house before I brought a friend home. She always did. This was around fourth or fifth grade.

Lest I sound too much like a spoiled brat, my brother, sister, and I had chores from as far back as I can remember. Every Saturday during the school year, we all had our bit to do—dusting, vacuuming, gathering up our things scattered around the house and putting them back in our bedrooms. My brother became a pro at cleaning the kitchen, especially messy pots and pans. I remember shaking Comet into the bathroom sink and tub now and again, scrubbing away with a damp sponge, probably ruining whatever kind of surface it was. When I was around eight, my mother showed me how to do laundry, fold clothes, change a bed, and set the table for dinner. During the summer, she taped to the refrigerator a daily rotation of chores among the three of us. My friend Jenny's mother did the same.

I think I was a senior in high school when my mother first hired a cleaning woman. Her name was Kate, and she came every two weeks. The night before she was due to arrive, my mother would spend considerable time straightening up the house, which I never understood. Now I know why. Before I clean my own house, I make sure things are put away and surfaces are clear, which makes it easier to dust. Kate was a single woman. I don't know whether she had children. I remember her as friendly and energetic, and she and my mother seemed to get along well. She had cats, like we did. My first summer out of college, when I had no job, she took me with her on a few cleaning jobs so I could earn a bit of cash. I remember going out to a McMansion one day.

Situated up a slope at the end of a long driveway, the huge brick house looked a little bereft. The development had yet to do any landscaping. There were no trees or shrubs anywhere, just dust and gravel. Inside, the house had, it seemed, dozens of rooms for this family of seven. I cleaned several bathrooms and then got a bit of a dressing down from the husband/father because I had left streaks on the chrome fixtures. I guess I got paid $10 or $15 an hour. Why did Kate take me with her? Did she really need the help? Or did my mother suggest it and she felt like she couldn't say no? A couple of years later, when my parents' cat, Cookie, started peeing in the house, Kate adopted her, a kind thing to do. I still feel terrible guilt about Cookie. My mother got her as a kitten when I was away at college and my parents were at work all day. I'm sure the tiny thing was desperately lonely. Once in a while, between classes, I would go home and play with her. She must have started peeing outside the litter box to get some attention. Kate gave her a happier home.

*****

My mother had various cleaning women or teams, including men, over the years. At first it was because she worked full-time and didn't want to spend all weekend on housework. Who could blame her? Shortly after she retired, she was diagnosed with rheumatoid arthritis and had myriad other issues over the years that rendered her less and less mobile. She couldn't physically clean a house on her own, let alone the large one she and my father had built after I graduated from college. Nevertheless, my mother experienced twinges of guilt over employing housekeepers. Perhaps not *white* liberal guilt, because all her cleaning crews were white, but guilt all the same. Over the years, she gave them possessions: housewares, décor, a bed frame and mattress, furniture, and boxes of books. I'm reminded of Woolf's Clarissa Dalloway thrusting one of her decorative pillows into her maid Lucy's arms on the morning of her party—a spontaneous gesture to show her appreciation but above all because she wants Lucy to like her. It mattered to Clarissa that she be liked by her servants. It mattered to my mother that she be liked by her cleaning crews.

My mother was friendly, kind, and generous. I presume her housekeepers did like her. As she became increasingly decrepit and unable to go up and down stairs much, some of them took advantage of her, though, especially where the finished basement was concerned. It was its own apartment, basically, with a TV room, bedroom, and full bath as well as a huge utility/storage room. When my husband and I would visit for a weekend or over the holidays, we usually stayed down there, and we began to see piles of dead bugs and cobwebs on windowsills and behind the nightstands. I would go upstairs and tell my mother she should ask her crew to clean and vacuum more thoroughly—move the furniture away from the walls to get at hard-to-reach areas, at least once in a while. But she wouldn't believe me, or she would say it was no big deal. I imagine she wanted to avoid confrontation. "It takes them three hours to clean the house," she'd say, as if it was an exorbitant amount of time. "It takes me three hours to clean my house," I'd tell her, "and it's half the size." I wasn't trying to be imperious. I just didn't want her taken advantage of.

I have never hired a cleaning woman. I'm able-bodied, perfectly capable of cleaning my own home. Certainly, I'd rather go for a walk or read or write on Saturday mornings, but I wouldn't be able to sit by or rove from room to room staying out of the way while someone else scrubbed our toilets. I would never want to hover and critique. I just can't do it. I cast no aspersions on those who do hire housekeepers and sometimes wonder if I'm making a mistake in not doing so myself. After all, everyone has to earn a living. Not everyone in domestic service is miserable or forced into it, are they? Yet in *Women, Race & Class*, Angela Davis deems domestic work "the least fulfilling of all employment." She advocates for its outsourcing to free housewives from the "[i]nvisible, repetitive, exhausting, unproductive, uncreative" drudgery of housework.

For many years now, businesses like Merry Maids, Molly Maid, and Two Maids & a Mop have been in high demand. Clearly, many people choose domestic work. But "choice" is a tricky word, never as simple as it seems. Is cleaning homes a "choice" for someone who would be unemployed otherwise? Is it a "choice" for immigrant women, undocumented women, women in this country who don't speak English, and women of color facing discrimination and limited employment opportunities? I remember overhearing two men at the gym talking to each to other about their cleaning women. One of them said he told "Maria" that unless he smelled bleach, he didn't consider anything clean. Her name was not Maria. It was obvious in the way he said it—exaggeratedly and with a smirk, and the way the two of them chuckled when he said it—that "Maria" was their catchword for a female domestic. Would I be doing a good thing by hiring a cleaning person and paying her or him well? Would my misgivings be assuaged if I hired a white person to clean my home? I suspect not. It just doesn't sit right with me. Friends in England tell me such handwringing about "servants" is a uniquely American phenomenon.

I'm not claiming moral high ground. I am, however, thinking of Sara Ahmed's essential book, *Living a Feminist Life*. Ahmed, like Davis before her, cites labor as a feminist matter. "Black women and women of color; working-class women; migrant women; women who have worked in the factories, in the fields, at home; women who care for their own children as well as other children; such women have become the arms for other women whose time and energy has been freed"—like Virginia Woolf and Vanessa Bell, free to write and paint in large part because domestic duties were undertaken by others their entire lives. "Any feminism that lives up to the promise of that name will not free some women from being arms by employing other women to take their place," Ahmed continues. "Feminism needs to refuse this division of labor, this freeing up of time and energy for some by the employment of the limbs of others. . . . A feminist army that gives life and vitality to some women's arms by taking life and vitality from other women's arms is reproducing inequality and injustice. That is not freedom." Alison Light states as much in the penultimate paragraph of *Mrs. Woolf and the Servants*: "*Cleaning is still the lowest-status job. And cleaners are predominantly women*" (original italics).

*****

In later years, Woolf assumed more household duties in part to ease her increasingly anxious mind. She became adept in the kitchen, learning a repertoire of dishes from her cooks. She baked a mean bread. When her home in Mecklenburgh Square was bombed during the Blitz, she battled the dirt and dust, beat the carpets, and salvaged as many books as she could. Toward the end of her life, she got down on her hands and knees and scrubbed her own floors, unheard of for a woman of her social class. Vanessa never would have done it. Their mother, Julia, would have been appalled. "As Virginia's mental state deteriorated Leonard himself suggested that she help Louie with the housework. Dusting had been good therapy at Asheham, all those years ago," Light writes. "But then, at Asheham, she had been in recovery, not breakdown. . . . And so Virginia spent her last morning dusting alongside Louie. After a while she put down her duster and went away," taking her final walk to the river.

Mrs. Woolf and the Servants spurred me to think for the first time in years about my mother's stance toward her housecleaners. She loved chatting with them, learning about their lives, meeting their children, and giving them things they might find useful or a pleasure to have. They in turn cared for her beloved home, made life easier for her, and kept her company when she was alone in the house while my father was still working and when she could no longer drive. I toast them and their brethren and continue to think about female labor, (in)equity, and the complexities of domestic service and space.

Chapter 6

When the Trees Say Nothing
by Thomas Merton

Kristin:
Get to know Thomas
Merton, the greatest spiritual
writer of the 20th century.
Dad

I've known the name Thomas Merton all my life. My father often mentioned him with great admiration. He used to tell us about reading *The Seven Storey Mountain*, Merton's spiritual autobiography, when he was in college and the enormous impact it had upon him. Although I knew only the bare bones of Merton's story, I knew that made sense. Catholic, scholar, writer, reader with a penchant for the outdoors, the colder and snowier the better—that was my father, who clearly shared commonalities with his idol. *Seven Storey Mountain* has been on my to-read list for many years. I haven't deliberately put it off. I've read bits of Merton over the years and always find him interesting and thought-provoking. It's just one of those things, I guess. If I live to be 100, I won't have time to read all the books in my house. Still, there may be more to it than that, which I realized while reading *When the Trees Say Nothing*, a collection of Merton's nature writings gathered from across his expansive oeuvre.

When the Trees Say Nothing came out in 2003, so I imagine my dad must have given it to me for Christmas that year. I was happy to receive it and looked forward to reading it, yet it sat on a shelf for 18 years before I got around to it, three years after my father died. At that point, I suppose I was primed for it. Amid political upheaval and the ongoing pandemic, I was seeking a means of reducing stress and anxiety. As 2021 sputtered to a close and the new year began, I vowed to turn away from screens and shut out noise as much as possible. I read Jaron Lanier's *Ten Arguments for Deleting Your Social Media Accounts Right Now*—and I did. I embarked on Dry January. I tried to meditate a few minutes each day. And I chose bedside reading that might calm and quiet my mind, including *When the Trees Say Nothing*. I also thought it was high time I became better acquainted with a writer who meant so much to my father. The book provided the balm for the soul I was hoping for, yet there were moments I could barely read through my tears.

*****

Editor Kathleen Deignan has divided the small, easy-to-hold-in-the-hand book into chapters on the seasons, elements, firmament (sky and clouds, sun and moon, planets and stars), creatures (from butterflies to rodents to deer to bees), festivals (rain, flowers, trees), presences (mountains), and sanctuary (forest). Thomas Berry writes in the Foreword that the "variety of Merton's experiences covers almost the entire panorama of the natural worlds available" to him in his decades in Kentucky, not far from where I write this in my home in the central part of the state. Merton recognized nature as "a mode of sacred presence primarily to be communed with in wonder and beauty and intimacy," Berry continues. His gift "is this sense of the sacred throughout the entire range of the natural world."

Merton entered the Trappist monastery of Gethsemani, near Bardstown, Kentucky, on December 10, 1941, when he was 26 years old. Ten years later, he requested greater solitude, where-upon "Abbot Dom James nominated him 'forester,'" as Deignan explains in her introduction, "which entailed restoring the woodlands that had been stripped a decade earlier." Along with tending the land and training novitiates, Merton read, wrote, and found peace and grace in the silence. A beautiful life, although not without its challenges. My father used to say that if my mother predeceased him, he would become a monk. In fact, he traveled to Gethsemani from time to time over the years for a retreat of solitude, contemplation, reading, and prayer, perhaps hoping to channel his hero in some way. At least, that's how I imagined it. I never really asked.

Chapters in *When the Trees Say Nothing* contain numbered passages of varying lengths, from single sentences to several pages—jottings made throughout the day or ruminations within essays on other topics, perhaps, noting the angle of the sun, the texture of the snow, and the feel of soft pine needles beneath bare feet. He describes the sounds he hears, like rain on the roof of his cabin, birdsong, and leaves rustling in the wind. He also writes of human-made noise, such as the drone of planes overhead from the Fort Knox military base or the whistling of a nearby train. Silence emerges as his most prevalent theme, however, along with his great respect for those who appreciate it, and for those who seek to dwell within it. "In the silence of the countryside and the forest, in the cloistered solitude of my monastery, I have discovered the whole Western Hemisphere," he declares.

Recounting his activities one late summer afternoon, he tells of "com[ing] down out of the novitiate, through the door in the wall, over the trestle and down into this green paradise of tall stalks and silence. I know the joy and the worship the Indians must have felt, and the Eucharistic rightness of it!" Although I wince at Merton's reference to Native peoples in the past tense—odd given that he explored, embraced, and wrote extensively about contemporary Indigenous spiritual practices—I can appreciate his sense of religious ecstasy in the forest. On another afternoon, feeling discouraged, he reorients himself as he sits on "a tree stump, in an even place. It was dry and a small cedar arched over it, like a green tent, forming an alcove. There I sat in silence and loved the wind in the forest and listened for a good while to God."

*****

Merton experiences the spiritual discernment that arises from immersion in the natural world. "The forms and individual characters of living and growing things, of inanimate beings, of animals and flowers and all nature, constitute their holiness in the sight of God. Their inscape," he writes, adopting a term coined by Gerard Manley Hopkins to mean the unique essence of a creature or natural structure, "is their sanctity. It is the imprint of His wisdom and His reality in them." Other passages show him relishing his role as forester, noting "How necessary it is for monks to work in the fields, in the rain, in the sun, in the mud, in the clay, in the wind . . . these are our spiritual directors and our novice-masters. They form our contemplation. They instill us with virtue. They make us as stable as the land we live in."

Of course, the land we live in bears the brunt of human intrusion, including our dubious means of obtaining knowledge. "There is something you cannot know about a wren by cutting it up in a laboratory," Merton states, a Wordsworthian pronouncement phrased so starkly, it takes my breath away. The only way to know the wren is if "it remains fully and completely a wren, itself, and hops on your shoulder if it feels like it." He also acknowledges the folly of his own environmental meddling in a passage worth quoting at length:

> The other day there was a beautiful whistling of titmice—and now today one of them lay dead on the grass under the house, which may well have been some fault of mine as we dumped some calcium chloride on a couple of anthills—not as a poison but as something to move them elsewhere. What a miserable bundle of foolish idiots we are! We kill everything around us even when we think we love and respect nature and life. This sudden power to deal death all around us *simply by the way we live*, and in total "innocence" and ignorance, is by far the most disturbing symptom of our time.

Such sentiments bring to mind Nikki Giovanni's poem "Allowables." "I killed a spider," she writes, "Not a murderous brown recluse / Nor even a black widow," merely a small "Sort of papery spider," but "she scared me / And I smashed her / I don't think / I'm allowed / To kill something / Because I am / Frightened." The poem's contemplative tone and accrual of shame and regret resonate with Merton's commentary on our thoughtless desecration of the natural world. At times, I was caught off guard by his disdain for humankind. "The clouds are high and enormous. In them, the inevitable jet plane passes," he observes, "this time probably full of fat passengers from Miami to Chicago, but presently it will be a plane with the bomb in it." Such passages stress the urgency of quelling our impulse to harm each other and the nonhuman others in our midst, who are themselves imbued with their own will and right to live. As Giovanni's title indicates, we must disallow such a mindset and create anew our sick, distracted, noisy consumer society. What would Merton think of today's climate crisis and the madness of social media?

*****

Above all, Merton dwells on the majesty of the natural world. Up and about before dawn each morning, he describes the awakening day in beautiful prose-poetry. "Sunrise: hidden by pines and cedars to the east: I saw the red flame of the kingly sun glaring through the black trees, not like dawn but like a forest fire. Then the sun became distinguished as a person and he shone silently and with solemn power through the branches, and the whole world was silent and calm." He also writes lyrically of the moon. "The moon was beautiful, dimly red like a globe of almost transparent amber, with a shapeless foetus of darkness curled in the midst of it. It hung there between two tall pines, silent, unexplained, small, with a modest suggestion of bloodiness, an omen without fierceness and without comment, pure." When was the last time I looked at the moon while outdoors? On clear nights, I peer up through our windows and exclaim over the moon's brightness and beauty, but I don't step outside to view it. I berate myself and promise I'll start.

I return to especially arresting ideas, such as, "The year struggles with its own blackness." He means it literally, noting dark skies and incessant rain that he contrasts with a bright New Year's Day. Yet I find the sentence an apt metaphor for the last five years in America. I read with pencil in hand and bracket especially lovely or thought-provoking passages. I stop short at one sentence in particular: "After None I sat in one of the windows of the Scriptorium . . . and watched the rain." After I graduated from college, my parents moved into a newly built house, and at long last, my father had a spacious home office all to himself. It had skylights, floor-to-ceiling bookshelves, a Persian rug, and a beautiful Amish-made desk. He dubbed the room the Scriptorium. I have no idea if he chose the name because of Merton, but seeing the word Scriptorium made me smile, and another piece of the puzzle clicked into place.

It's clear from Merton's nature writings that he travelled quite a bit. He notes shadows cast by buildings on the pavement in New York City. He mentions New Mexico many times and the vistas of coastal California. I envy his travel, his profound knowledge of the woods, birds, and animals, and his rising before dawn to feel the air and wind, and to gaze at the starlit sky. Several times, he mentions both the serenity and the excitement of sheltering under a tree during a rainstorm. When I was a kid, my friends and I used to rush outside during downpours and turn our faces up to the sky. We'd play games in the rain and run around laughing, getting soaked to the bone. Why did we ever stop?

Interested in knowing more about Merton, I head to the internet. I learn that he died by accidental electrocution on December 10, 1968, in Bangkok—27 years to the day after he entered Gethsemani. He was 53 years old and had traveled to Bangkok to continue his studies in eastern spiritual traditions. Some theories hold that he was assassinated due to his opposition to the Vietnam War. Others say he may have had a heart attack. Suddenly, a passage from *When the Trees Say Nothing* assumes a haunting new significance. "Clear, thin new moon appearing and disappearing blue clouds—and the living black skeletons of the trees against the evening sky. More artillery than usual whumping at Knox. It is my fifty-third birthday." He has less than a year to live.

*****

A December 2018 *New Yorker* profile of Merton recounts his problematic early years. He went to Cambridge University, drank to excess, landed in and out of jail, and fathered a child he never met. He was eventually expelled and went on to Columbia University, where he found his vocation. "He was his contradictions," writes Alan Jacobs in "Thomas Merton: The Monk Who Became a Prophet": "the person in motion who seeks stillness; the monk who wants to belong to the world; the famous person who wants to be unknown. . . . He sought the peace of pure and silent contemplation, but came to believe that the value of that experience is to send us back into the world that killed us." Maybe he would have gravitated toward social media more than I initially imagined, for "He is perhaps the proper patron saint of our information-saturated age," Jacobs goes on, "of we who live and move and have our being in social media, and then, desperate for peace and rest, withdraw into privacy and silence, only to return. As we always will." Merton recognized his contradictions. "To be conscious of both extremes of my solitary life," he muses; "consolation and desolation; understanding, obscurity; obedience and protest; freedom and imprisonment."

This issue of *The New Yorker* came out on December 18, 2018, three days before my father died. I wish he could have read it. He would have loved it and would surely have recommended that I read it, too—and I would have. We could have talked about the article together, and perhaps then I would have asked him to tell me more about Merton's influence upon him, about his visits to Gethsemani, and about any other topics that might have arisen. But it was not to be.

At the start of this essay, I claimed to have eagerly opened *When the Trees Say Nothing*. That's true. At the same time, I read it with trepidation as I knew it would trigger an emotional whirlwind—and so it did. Over and over, one question clanged and wailed in my head: "Why didn't I read this, and *Seven Storey Mountain*, years ago when Dad was alive so that we could talk about them together?" Once I go down that rabbit hole, I find it hard to climb out. I then remember other things, like his telling me, all my life, that his favorite movie was *How Green Was My Valley*, a 1941 film about a Welsh mining family. Such a description did little to entice me back in the day, and I never watched it. Still haven't. Why not? Would it have killed me to sit down with my dad and roll the movie? He would have been delighted. Since he died, all the *could haves* and *should haves* have stacked up into a tall, menacing tower.

*****

Born and raised in Green Bay, Wisconsin, my father relished the cold and snow. When our family woke up on the morning of January

26, 1978, to more than two feet of snow on the ground, he was like a kid in a candy store. He was so excited and couldn't wait to get outside, where he walked and shoveled and hiked for hours and hours each day over the next few weeks. That may have been the winter he took a hose to our backyard and made an ice rink for us. Every day, my brother, sister, and I skated and played hockey until it grew too dark out to see. I think of the snowy days at my parents' house over the holidays when I was an adult and all the times my father and I could have gone for a walk together. I had so many opportunities to get to know him better, and I stupidly, selfishly let them slip through my fingers. These are the thoughts that have me on my knees howling into the abyss.

I expressed as much in an email to my friend Erica when she asked why I was writing about Merton. I treasure her insightful and sensitive response. "I can imagine you've told yourself this before," she wrote in an email, "but I will attempt it in my own words anyway. You have Thomas Merton now so that you can still be in conversation with your father. You didn't need these books when your father was alive because you had your father. You need his writing now as a way to be with your dad in his physical absence perhaps? A shallow consolation, I am sure, but that is immediately what came to mind when I read your email. In fact, Merton's words are likely your father's way of providing comfort to you in this time of personal grief and global uncertainty." I hold these reassuring sentiments close as I think of my parents, delve deeper into Merton, and learn a bit about Buddhist teachings on death, grief, and the importance of self-compassion.

Dry January didn't take, and I'm back on Twitter (*only to return... as we always will*), but tomorrow is another day—and one day, I will read *The Seven Storey Mountain* and strive to learn and grow from it as I have from *When the Trees Say Nothing*. I would hate for the books my mother and father loved to become totems of regret and remorse. Instead, I can appreciate them as benevolent presences beckoning from the shelves, inviting me to commune with my parents by reading what they read, and to feel them within and around me.

Chapter 7

Wuthering Heights
by Emily Brontë
Jane Eyre
by Charlotte Brontë

To Kristin
for her 14th Christmas
Read with delight and
pleasure, my dear.
Love, forever and ever
Dad   1983

As I opened this volume, thoughts rushed through my head like winds sweeping over the moors. First among them was that my father had once held this book in his hands. I read his inscription several times, passing my fingertips over the ink. I imagined him selecting the book and considering how to inscribe it before handing it to my mother to wrap and place under the Christmas tree. I thought of my mother's Anglophilia and the Victorian touches in our home. Framed pictures hung close together on living room walls. A silver tea set, polished to gleaming perfection. Delicate floral teacups and saucers on the shelves of her secretary. And I can see the orange Penguin spines of her Anthony Trollope novels taking up an entire bookshelf. I thought of Sylvia Plath and her husband, Ted Hughes, who lived for a time in Devon in a cottage near Top Withens, purportedly Emily Brontë's inspiration for the setting of *Wuthering Heights*. Plath and Hughes enjoyed walking to Top Withens and visiting the Brontë Parsonage, and they likened themselves to Catherine and Heathcliff as they rambled over the moors. Like Brontë's doomed couple and the Brontës themselves, Sylvia and Ted were also destined for a legendary afterlife.

I made my own pilgrimage to the Brontës' Haworth Parsonage in June 2004 during a trip to see my friend Traci in York. I took the train to visit her after attending the annual Virginia Woolf conference in London, memorable for many reasons, top among them meeting Leonard and Virginia Woolf's nephew, Cecil Woolf, and his wife, the writer Jean Moorcroft Wilson, with whom, to my utter astonishment and delight, I would become friends. Arriving in York, I asked Traci if a trip to Haworth would be doable, and indeed it was. The day of our excursion happened to coincide with the 150th wedding anniversary of Charlotte Brontë and Arthur Bell Nicholls. We attended a reenactment of their wedding in the church, and Haworth residents roamed about in period clothing. It was a magical day, and grim, for we also learned of Haworth's mortality rates during the time of the Brontës—rates so atrocious, Patrick Brontë insisted upon an investigation of the matter, undertaken by Benjamin Hershel Babbage in 1850.

Hair-raising sanitary conditions were to blame. As Blake Morrison writes in his *Guardian* article on the public's never-ending fascination with the Brontës, "with no drains or running water, disease was rife—the average life expectancy in Haworth at that time was 28.5 years." The custom of installing tombstones flat on the ground also led to death and disease. "Beneath the large markers lying on the ground deep pits were dug," writes Jeff Minick, "and as family members died, their casket would be placed atop those below and the slab replaced. What the folk of that time did not understand was that the slabs kept oxygen from the earth, and the slowly rotting flesh was close to the water supply." Emily Temple puts it bluntly in her *Literary Hub* piece on the subject: The Brontës "spent their lives drinking water contaminated by the local graveyard—and possibly the local privies, too." Once Babbage ascertained the problem, "Patrick Brontë insisted on upright tombstones," Minick explains, "and he planted trees in the cemetery to speed the process of decomposition."

I made a second trip to Haworth in 2016 on the front end of that year's Woolf conference, held at Leeds-Trinity University. A busload of jetlagged but eager Woolfians rode over on a cool, drizzly spring day and enjoyed an exclusive presentation by the Brontë Parsonage Museum director. We then clustered in a reverential hush around the visitor guestbook to see Woolf's signature in her maiden name, Virginia Stephen, from her long-ago visit to

Haworth with her friend, Margaret Vaughan. Her ensuing essay, "Haworth, November 1904," was one of her first publications. She loved that the town of Keighley, four miles from Haworth, was still like "the Keighley of [Charlotte's] day," all the easier to "picture the slight figure of Charlotte trotting along the streets in her thin mantle, hustled into the gutter by more burley pass-ers-by." She paid homage in the Brontë house and navigated the crowded graveyard. "[T]he stones seem to start out of the ground at you in tall, upright lines, like an army of silent soldiers. There is no handsbreadth untenanted." In the church, she gazed at "the slab which bears the names of the succession of [Brontë] children and their parents—their births and deaths." Words beneath the names give thanks to God "which giveth the victory through our Lord Jesus Christ." Virginia Stephen deemed it an apt inscription, "for however harsh the struggle, Emily, and Charlotte above all, fought to victory."

I visited Traci and her family, now living in Sheffield, after the Leeds-Trinity conference as well. Before flying to England, I emailed her and asked if we could visit Sylvia Plath's grave in Heptonstall, just nine miles from Haworth, after she picked me up at my hotel when the conference was over. She told me she had already bought us all tickets to a professional cricket match. I had to admit that sounded like a more enjoyable way to spend a Sunday afternoon.

*****

As I have so many times before, I devoured *Wuthering Heights* and *Jane Eyre* when I read them to gear up for writing this essay. Like readers around the world for nearly two hundred years, I was captivated by the intricate plotlines, complex characters, and descriptions of the natural world. Emily and Charlotte knew every inch of the moors—their flora, fauna, and weather throughout the seasons, and their caprices and moods as well. Yet I struggled with intertwining anxieties as I read that threatened to impede my full immersion in the stories. My old nemesis, Impostor Syndrome, had sidled up to remind me that I would eventually have to at-tempt the impossible: write something new and interesting about these novels. The gall to believe I could do such a thing! Harold

Bloom coined the term "anxiety of influence" for the pressure authors feel to write something original while bearing the weight of all the writing that came before them. Is there a similar term for readers? What do we do with all the literature crowding our brains? How do we sort it? Or does it defy organization and slosh around like water at the bottom of a leaky boat? Either way, we have no choice but to accept the assemblage of words, scenes, and images accrued over a lifetime that orbit our minds as we read.

These musings rang a bell. Searching through old files, I found a conference paper from 2008 in which I addressed similar issues. "My presentation today explores the early letters of Virginia Woolf," the paper begins, "the first of the six volumes of letters, covering the years 1888 to 1912, when Virginia Woolf was still Virginia Stephen . . . My concern today is how we might read the letters of Virginia Stephen without burdening them with all we know of Virginia Woolf's life and writing." All these years later, I had come full circle, but with the Brontës instead of Woolf.

In standard academese, my conference paper provided a run-down of various theories of reading. Embarking on *Wuthering Heights* and *Jane Eyre*, I again heard the siren song of research. I brought the Norton Critical Edition of each novel home from my campus office and intended to read their introductions and excerpts from scholarly sources. There the books sat, next to my desk, taunting me until I reminded myself of what I set out to do in this project: read the books inscribed and given to me by my parents for pure enjoyment, free of expectations. Another intention, though, was to follow any pathways that opened up as I read. So I resisted the Nortons but turned to Woolf's essay "*Jane Eyre* and *Wuthering Heights*," published in 1916, marveling as always at her gift for discerning the essence of a writer and her work. "[A]ll her force," she says of Charlotte, "and it is the more tremendous for being constricted, goes into the assertion, 'I love,' 'I hate,' 'I suffer'." "She could free life from its dependence on facts," she writes of Emily; "with a few touches indicate the spirit of a face so that it needs no body, by speaking of the moor make the wind blow and the thunder roar."

Even Woolf is fallible, though. In her *Atlantic* article on the Brontës, Judith Shulevitz claims Woolf missed the mark when she stated in *A Room of One's Own* that Charlotte Brontë compromised *Jane Eyre* by imbuing her eponymous character with anger about women's circumscribed lot in life, for "if one reads [her pages] over and marks that jerk in them, that indignation," Woolf writes, "one sees that she will never get her genius expressed whole and entire. Her books will be deformed and twisted. She will write in a rage where she should write calmly. She will write foolishly where she should write wisely. ... She is at war with her lot. How could she help but die young, cramped and thwarted? One could not but play for a moment with the thought of what might have happened if Charlotte Brontë had possessed say three hundred a year."

"But Woolf gets it exactly wrong," Shulevitz states, and I have read enough by and about both Woolf and the Brontës to concur. "The sisters' social and economic disadvantages didn't hold them back. Charlotte and Emily explored—and exploited—the prison-house of gender with unprecedented clear-sightedness." Their brief, ill-fated "forays into the marketplace of female labor gave them their best material," Shulevitz asserts. Woolf would go on to express an altogether different stance on anger, deploying it to spectacular effect in her feminist, pacifist work, *Three Guineas*. Perhaps by that time she had changed her mind about anger in *Jane Eyre* as well.

Anne Carson's "The Glass Essay" arose next in my mind, her remarkable poem/lyric essay in which she reflects on the end of a relationship, her efforts to recover, and her aging parents, all through the lens of Emily Brontë's poetry and prose—though not without misgivings. "I fear I am turning into Emily Brontë," Carson writes, "my lonely life around me like a moor, / my ungainly body stumping over the mud flats with a look of / transformation / that dies when I come in the kitchen door. / What meat is it, Emily, we need?" Although Emily's biographers insist on the "fact" of her unremarkable life, Carson senses something far more visceral at play. "The little raw soul was caught by no one," she states. "She didn't have friends, children, sex, religion, marriage, success, a / salary / or a fear of death . . . Yet her poetry from beginning to end is concerned with prisons, / vaults, cages, bars, curbs, bits, bolts, fetters, / locked windows, narrow frames, aching walls. . . .

'What was this cage, invisible to us, / which she felt herself to be confined in,'" the critics ask. "Well," Carson reflects, "there are many ways of being held prisoner." She imagines the possible sources of Emily's anger and whether "anger could be a kind of vocation for some women." How else explain the wrath of Heathcliff, the fury in her poetry?

Carson strikes a devastating note in "On Charlotte," a Short Talk from *Plainwater* that quotes part of a letter written by long-time Brontë family servant Martha Brown after the deaths of Emily and Anne. Reflecting on the sisters' nightly routine of walking around the kitchen table discussing their stories and novels, Martha writes/ Carson quotes, "Miss Emily walked as long as she could, and when she died, Miss Anne & Miss Brontë took it up—and now my heart aches to hear Miss Brontë walking, walking on alone." Tears spring to my eyes whenever I read these lines, though I have read them dozens of times, just as my heart rises into my throat upon reading the fifth bracket in the "Time Passes" section of Woolf's *To the Lighthouse*: "[Mr. Ramsay, stumbling along a passage one dark morning, stretched his arms out, but Mrs. Ramsay, having died rather suddenly the night before, his arms, though stretched out, remained empty.]" In a swirl of associations, the trauma of Mrs. Ramsay's death evokes the collected Brontë letters, every bit as absorbing as the novels. There's sad, I thought when I read them for the first time, and then there's Charlotte-writing-about-the-deaths-of-all-three-siblings-within-eight-months sad.

*****

Writers of all stripes have fallen under the Brontës' spell, evident in the hundreds of biographies, critical studies, graphic and illustrated works—even a series called The Brontë Sisters for Babies and Children. Prequels, sequels, and dozens of novels take up the lives and works in one way or another. Caryl Phillips's *The Lost Child* provides Heathcliff with a backstory. Alison Case's *Nelly Dean: A Return to Wuthering Heights* expands the role of that novel's principal narrator. In Catherine Lowell's *The Madwoman Upstairs: A Novel of the Last Brontë*, a female university student becomes embroiled in a hunt for a rumored Brontë estate. Brontë-inspired poetry includes Rita Maria Martinez's *The Jane and Bertha in Me*. In her 1961 poem "Wuthering Heights," Sylvia Plath contemplates the alluring, somewhat ominous moors, where sheep "stand about in grandmotherly disguise, / All wig curls and yellow teeth / and hard, marbly baas." And of course, there's the crème de la crème, Jean Rhys's *Wide Sargasso Sea*.

Saddened and bemused by the depiction in *Jane Eyre* of the Creole woman, Rochester's first wife, Jean Rhys, Creole herself, transformed Charlotte's snarling, animalistic "Bertha" into a character of depth, nuance, and poignancy. In *Wide Sargasso Sea*, Antoinette Cosway Mason tells of her lonely childhood, her troubled mother, her arranged marriage to an Englishman whose father and brother seek to rob him of his patrimony, their brief period of happiness, how it all went to hell, and finally, her imprisonment in the attic of Thornfield Hall until her death by suicide, leaping from the ramparts after setting the manor on fire. Rochester, unnamed in the novel, gets to speak his piece as well. In fact, it wasn't until the Rochester character assumed a voice that the novel finally coalesced, as Carole Angier explains in her biography of Rhys. "Another 'I' must talk, two others perhaps," Rhys wrote in a letter of 1958. "Then the Creole's 'I' will come to life." Angier attributes Rhys's eventual breakthrough to her life-long love of poetry. "In early April [1964] she wrote four poems," Angier explains. "But it was the fourth poem that was important. It was called 'Obeah Night.' In it Jean became Edward Rochester: and when she did that her long battle with the novel was won."

Hard won. Rhys worked on *Wide Sargasso Sea* in fits and starts for nearly a decade, possibly longer, primarily in her dilapidated cottage in the Devon village of Cheriton Fitzpaine, where she moved with her third husband, Max Hamer, in 1960. Angier delves into the long slog that was the writing of *Wide Sargasso Sea* and the unlikely hero who helped see it through: the vicar of Cheriton Fitzpaine, the Rev. Alwynne Woodard. When Rhys's brother, Edward Rees Williams, installed his troublesome sister in Devon, he paid the vicar a visit "both to warn Mr. Woodard and to ask him to help her." In the end, Mr. Woodward would offer much more than pastoral care, "[f]or Alwynne Woodard was also a scholar, and in particular a lover of literature." Jean trusted him and told him she was a writer—but a thwarted one "because of

Max's illness, because of poverty; but also because she was just stuck. . . . she told him that she'd thrown the book away."

One day when Woodard arrived at the cottage, he found Rhys "drunk and ill, huddled in bed." What happens next gives me goosebumps. Angier recreates the scenario:

> he made up his mind to look for the book. At first he must have thought there wasn't one after all, or that she'd thrown it away as she'd said for there was no normal pile of note-books or paper on any of the tables. But then he must have seen a piece of paper sticking out somewhere; and suddenly he saw pieces of paper everywhere, covered with squiggles and scrawls. He retrieved them—from plastic bags and hat boxes, from under the bed and the sofa, from on top of the wardrobes and inside kitchen cupboards. He put them all together and took them home. He asked his daughter Helen to help him: together they spread out all the bits of paper they could on the big Rectory table. Luckily some pages at least were numbered, and a core of order began to emerge.

I imagine Rev. Woodard got goosebumps, too, for he knew he had a work of genius on his hands. He went to Rhys's cottage every day to help her stay focused, organized, and comfortable. "He understood her perfectly. 'She needs endless supplies of whisky, and endless praise, . . . so that is what she must have,'" Angier quotes him as saying. Andre Deutsch published *Wide Sargasso Sea* in 1966, a watershed moment in the literary world, for along with being a masterpiece in and of itself, Jean's novel works an alchemy on Charlotte's. It *changes* it. No one who reads *Wide Sargasso Sea* can ever read *Jane Eyre* the same way again—certainly not its characterization of Bertha, the woman who must die so that Jane may utter what would become one of the most famous lines in all of literature: "Reader, I married him."

It dawns on me that Jean Rhys and Sylvia Plath overlapped in Devon for more than a year. North Tawton, where Plath lived, and Cheriton Fitzpaine are just 18 miles apart. There's no evidence that they ever crossed paths, but Miranda Seymour, in her new biography of Rhys, offers the tantalizing fact that

Rhys read Ted Hughes's poetry and "was a greater admirer of the self-laceratingly honest work of his first wife, Sylvia Plath." In addition, Plath scholar Amanda Golden shared with me that Plath filled out a survey for poets in the February 1962 issue of *The London Magazine*, the same issue that carried Rhys's short story "Let Them Call it Jazz." I don't think it's far-fetched to presume that Plath read it. If so, perhaps it resonated with her, living in the thick of Brontë country, for the main character of "Jazz," Selina Davis, bears traces of Rhys's Antoinette, who was born of Charlotte's Bertha.

A biracial West Indian immigrant living in London, Selina Davis suffers persecution from her white English neighbors, the police, and predatory men due to her poverty, skin color, and West Indian patois. Unable to pay a fine after she's brought up on charges for breaking her neighbors' window, she serves a stint in Holloway Prison—as Rhys once did after repeated altercations with her neighbors. The story ends on an upbeat note as Selina experiences a renewed sense of self despite the theft of a song she wrote by a white male musician. The sum of her experiences, including incarceration, as a West Indian woman in a cold, hostile England evokes those of Antoinette in *Wide Sargasso Sea*. The publication timeline shows the two characters co-existing in Rhys's mind—displaced, maltreated but spirited Creole women for the nineteenth and twentieth centuries. I can picture Plath reading "Let Them Call it Jazz." And I like to imagine her and Rhys, just a stone's throw away from each other, writing by the dawn light streaming into their Devon cottages.

And so, what was meant to be an essay on *Wuthering Heights* and *Jane Eyre* becomes one on women readers and writers engaging each other across space and time, "for we look back through our mothers, if we are women," Woolf declares in *A Room of One's Own*. Connections arise everywhere. As Susan Orlean explains regarding her decision to write *The Library Book*, "if something you learn or observe or imagine can be set down and saved, and if you can see your life reflected in previous lives, and can imagine it reflected in subsequent ones, you can begin to discover order and harmony. You know that you are a part of a larger story that has shape and purpose." Do I fit somewhere into this larger story of women readers and writers? Is it all right to throw in my own two cents about the Brontë novels? Why am I asking permission, and from whom? Why not simply forge ahead?

*****

As I began reading *Wuthering Heights*, Catherine Earnshaw's passion for books and compulsion to write stood out more starkly than in previous readings. In the novel's opening pages, Lockwood finds a stack of books in the bedroom at the Heights where he's been grudgingly installed by Heathcliff for the night while a winter storm rages. He opens several crumbly volumes to find that someone named Catherine has annotated and doodled in them. In fact, she seems to have written every chance she got in diaries as well as in the books she read. "I shut, and took up another, and another, till I had examined all," Lockwood says. "Catherine's library was select; and its state of dilapidation proved it to have been well used, though not altogether for a legitimate purpose; scarcely one chapter had escaped a pen and ink commentary—at least, the appearance of one—covering every morsel of blank that the printer had left." Later, books cement the bond between Cathy Linton and Hareton Earnshaw, for Cathy makes peace with the young man she had taunted for his illiteracy by offering to teach him to read. As I read *Wuthering Heights* this time around, I enjoyed tracking scenes involving books, reading, and writing.

Heathcliff's brutal treatment of women emerges as a far less palatable theme. While I had always been appalled by his cruelty, I now found it especially hard to bear. No doubt the #MeToo Movement had awakened an even greater sensitivity to the novel's frequent scenes of domestic abuse and intimate partner violence. Heathcliff's tormenting of his wife, Isabella, is particularly monstrous. In a long letter to Nelly Dean several weeks after marrying Heathcliff, Isabella divulges her husband's physical, psychological, and emotional abuse. She finally escapes him, running off during a sudden spring snowfall, penniless and pregnant—a circumstance almost too grim to contemplate. Given Heathcliff's contempt for his wife, and her hatred and fear of him, one can only surmise that their coupling was rough at best, rape at worst. As in the past, I could also barely stand to read of Heathcliff's holding Nelly Dean and Cathy Linton captive in his house to force Cathy to marry his sickly son, Linton, and to prevent her from returning to Thrushcross Grange to tend her dying father. The tension builds to an unbearable pitch—testimony to Emily's skill along with my anxiety in the face of strife and frustration.

Heathcliff's violence extends to animals—or maybe it began with animals as is often the case with abusers—most notably when he hangs Isabella's dog, Fanny, whom Nelly rescues after happening upon her strangling, dangling from a fence. The novel is far more disturbing than film adaptations would have us believe, for they generally paint Heathcliff as a handsome, brooding Byronic hero with a hidden but profound capacity for love. Yet as Catherine admonishes Isabella when she fancies herself in love with Heathcliff, "Pray, don't imagine that he conceals depths of benevolence and affection beneath a stern exterior! He's not a rough diamond—a pearl-containing oyster of a rustic; he's a fierce, pitiless, wolfish man. . . . and he'd crush you, like a sparrow's egg, Isabella, if he found you a troublesome charge." Emily Brontë's insights into the dark realms of human nature are not for the faint of heart. Mercifully, humanity and goodness break through at times as in the growing love between Cathy and Hareton as the story draws to a close. Finally, I thought, a chance to exhale and know the next generation will set things right.

Jane Eyre has no shortage of its own miserable characters: Jane's Reed relations, who render her an outcast in their home; Mr. Brocklehurst, the cruel, hypocritical superintendent of Lowood School; the snooty Blanche Ingram, who detests Jane for her hold on Rochester's affections; and the insufferable St. John Rivers, who bullies Jane with his verbosity and the silent treatment alike. Throughout the novel, I admire Jane's presence of mind and determination to sit calmly with her thoughts, assess her circumstances, and gauge her emotions before making her next move, whether responding to one of the insults lobbed her way or deciding to leave Thornfield Hall when confronted with the fact of Rochester's wife. I love her contemplative turn of mind, her sense of self, her guilelessness, and her kindness and compassion toward people I would have junk-heaped at the first opportunity.

I respect Jane's intelligence and envy her exquisite—and often very funny—turns of phrase, as when the guests at Thornfield

Hall awaken and panic upon hearing a blood-curdling scream in the middle of the night. "'What awful event has taken place?' said [Miss Ingram.] 'Speak! Let us know the worst at once!' 'But don't pull me down or strangle me,' [Rochester] replied; for the Misses Eshton were clinging about him now, and the two dowagers, in vast white wrappers, were bearing down on him like ships in full sail." Jane's eye for detail and gift for vivid description keep me invested in her story. "It was not a bright or splendid summer evening, though fair and soft," she observes upon departing Thornfield to tend to her dying Aunt Reed:

> the haymakers were at work all along the road; and the sky, though far from cloudless, was such as promised well for the future: its blue—where blue was visible—was mild and settled, and its cloud strata high and thin. The west, too, was warm; no watery gleam chilled it—it seemed as if there was a fire lit, an altar burning behind its screen of marbled vapour, and out of apertures shone a golden redness.

I exult in such beautifully rendered scenes.

And I commiserate with Jane during her early days at Lowood, which Charlotte modeled on Cowan Bridge School, where she and her sisters briefly resided when they were little girls. In the spring of 1824, Patrick enrolled Maria, Elizabeth, Charlotte, and Emily at Cowan, where deprivation and contagion were the norm. Maria contracted tuberculosis there and died at home on May 6, 1825, age 11. Elizabeth died of the same disease five weeks later at age 10. Patrick rushed back to Cowan Bridge to retrieve Charlotte and Emily lest they meet the same fate. I held my breath as Jane described the rampant sickness and death at Lowood—the same conditions that destroyed Charlotte's sisters and that account in no small part for the world's fascination with her family. "That forest dell, where Lowood lay, was the cradle of fog and fog-bred pestilence," Jane recounts, "which, quickening with the quickening spring, crept into the Orphan Asylum, breathed typhus through its crowded schoolroom and dormitory, and, ere May arrived, transformed the seminary into a hospital." The mild, beautiful spring days belie the horrors inside Lowood.

What must it have taken for Charlotte to reflect on the suffering and deaths of her sisters, to write the horrors of Cowan Bridge in such meticulous detail? She also recreated her sister Maria in the character of Jane's closest Lowood friend, Helen Burns—saintly, mistreated by sadistic teachers, then ill and dying in the middle of the night as Jane sleeps by her side. In the novel, typhus, not tuberculosis, spreads throughout the school, reminding me of the typhus that ravaged Virginia Stephen's family when her beloved brother Thoby died of the disease in 1906, at age 26. He had contracted typhus on the Stephen siblings' trip to Greece, and for several weeks after he died, Virginia pretended he was still alive in letters to her friend Violet Dickinson, who was also ill at the time and whom Virginia didn't wish to distress with news of the death.

On November 22, two days after Thoby's death, she writes to Violet, "Thoby is as well as possible. We aren't anxious." On November 25: "Thoby is going on splendidly. He is very cross with his nurses, because they wont give him mutton chops and beer; and he asks why he cant go for a ride with Bell, and look for wild geese." In early December: "Thoby is more hungry but healthy and rather better they say. I suppose he cant get stronger till he eats. These dreary details you will supply for yourself. They say his attack must have been worse than yours as his temp. was so high, but its a thing that leaves no ill effects—indeed it recoats your inside—so you can look forward to a double life in purity and cleanliness."

Virginia wrote 18 such letters, through December 17, when Violet learned the truth by accident. "Beloved Violet, Do you hate me for telling so many lies?" she writes on December 18. She extends sympathy, trying to comfort Violet about Thoby's death rather than seek comfort from her. "These great things are not terrible, and I know we can still make a good job of it—and we want you more and more. . . . You are part of all that is best, and happiest in our lives. Thoby was always asking about you. I know you loved him, and he loved you. The only thing I feel I could not bear would be to think that this news should make you worse. . . . Beloved, get well and come back to your Wall who loves you." Woolf would write about Thoby for the rest of her life—in the character of Jacob Flanders in *Jacob's Room* and Percival in *The Waves*, for instance—promising young men dead before their time. Having written a book about a deceased sibling in my own family, I like to think of Charlotte and Virginia as kindred spirits, memorializing in writing our lost sisters and brothers. "You're bringing her back to life," my father wrote to me after reading a draft of my book. "What a wonderful exercise in the recovery of memory! And what a great gift you have given to your parents."

I wish I could tell my father how much I treasure his gift of the Brontës. I wish my mother and I could have visited Haworth together. The memories and chains of association that arise from writing about the books my parents gave me enable me to hold them close in a way I would not have thought possible. I think again of Susan Orlean's *Library Book*. "In Senegalese," she explains, "the polite expression for saying someone died is to say his or her library has burned." She puzzles over the phrase before concluding that "it was perfect. Our minds and souls contain volumes inscribed by our experiences and emotions; each individual's consciousness is a collection of memories we've cataloged and stored inside us, a private library of a life lived. . . . if you can take something from that internal collection and share it—with one person or with the larger world, on the page or in a story recited—it takes on a life of its own"—as does each of my parent-inscribed books, full of life and greatly cherished.

Chapter 8

The Love of a Good Woman: Stories
by Alice Munro

To Kristin
from Mom
Merry Christmas, 1998

I had a professor in graduate school tell the class one night that she never read short stories. That the short story was a sub-par genre. That only those who couldn't hack writing a novel resorted to the short story. I don't remember whether she elaborated on these opinions, but I do remember being aghast—and somewhat abashed, because I love short stories, and because this professor intimidated me even while I admired her and enjoyed her class. "What about Joyce?" one student asked. "Well, Joyce may be an exception," she replied. I should have piped up, too. "What about Chekhov? What about Virginia Woolf? William Trevor? Louise Erdrich? Alice Munro?" For a while in the early 2000s, *The New Yorker* settled into a rotation of stories by Trevor, Erdrich, and Munro. Bliss! I hope that in all my years of teaching, I never made students feel embarrassed about who or what they read. And I wonder why, given her antipathy toward the form, this professor had us read *East, West*, a collection of short stories by Salman Rushdie. I think she must have enjoyed being contrarian.

My mother gave me *The Love of a Good Woman*, by Alice Munro, for Christmas in 1998. It's a hefty book, a collection of eight stories totaling over 300 pages. As I began rereading it recently, I paused for a moment and thought about how my mother had surely read it as well, for she loved Alice Munro. I envisioned her holding the book in her hands just like I was, an image recalling the final words of Toni Morrison's *Jazz*. As the novel draws to a close, the narrator describes the intimacy between couples who have grown old together and weathered many storms: their private "undercover whispers" as well as their open expressions of love—a glance, a gesture, a casual running of fingertips over a sleeve to grab a bit of lint. "I envy them their public love," the narrator says, having only experienced secret love that could not be spoken aloud.

Yet she yearns to give voice to her love. "If I were able I'd say it. Say make me, remake me. You are free to do it and I am free to let you because look, look. Look where your hands are. Now"— words expressing the physicality entwined in such a declaration of love as well as the vulnerability of divulging such thoughts. These words compel the reader to look at her own hands holding the book. To be present in the act of reading. To be invested in the story, understanding of the characters, and in dialogue with the author so that we come out on the other side with new insights that alter the contours of who we are. The concluding words of *Jazz* also remind us of our own creative capacities as we make and remake the stories we read and return to. As we are never the same moment to moment, neither are the books we read. I used to tell my students the words inside a book are meaningless until a human being opens it up and begins to engage with them—that we all possess the potential for story-making.

My mother sitting in a chair holding a book in her hands forms the background, and foreground, of my entire life. After she died and I began wearing her wedding ring, I noticed that our hands are exactly alike.

*****

The title story of *The Love of a Good Woman* runs nearly 80 pages, more like a novella than a short story. In the beginning, young boys happen upon the body of the local optometrist inside his car, submerged in a lake. Did he drown in the car after an accident, or did he meet with foul play? The boys don't know, and when they return to their homes for dinner that afternoon, they

72

remain mum. We're then given a window into each boy's family. Cece Ferns has a downtrodden mother, an abusive alcoholic father, and a "hiding place he had made outside the house in the blind corner past the dining-room window." Bud Salter has a younger brother along with "two older sisters who never did anything useful unless his mother made them." Jimmy Box lives with his siblings, mother, and "crippled" father "in his grandmother's house with his grandmother and his great-aunt Mary and his bachelor uncle." After spending a bit more time with the boys, the story pivots to a character named Enid and remains with her for the duration. In such a manner, Munro establishes the interconnectedness among people, though they never cross paths, and the complexity of lives young and old.

I didn't remember anything about the story until about forty pages in, when I experienced déjà vu—an overwhelming sensation but one so fleeting, I couldn't pinpoint its source before it dissipated and flitted out of reach. Munro provides Enid's backstory at this point—how a bright young woman living with her widowed mother occupies her time, and how she became a caregiver for the sick and infirm in their small town. Something on this page struck me as familiar, especially its last sentence: "Her hope was to be good, and do good, and not necessarily in the orderly, customary, wifely way," which makes sense as Munro's women characters are rarely orderly, customary, or wifely. We learn that Enid cares for a Mrs. Quinn, a twenty-something mother of two young girls who is slowly, agonizingly dying.

One day, Mrs. Quinn divulges to Enid that before she became ill, she had been repeatedly sexually assaulted by the local optometrist, Mr. Willens. "I could tell you something you wouldn't believe," she says. The horrible details spew forth, but Mrs. Quinn has grown so angry and mean in her illness, Enid isn't sure what to believe. She then hears about the day Mr. Quinn happened upon Willens hiking up his wife's skirt during an eye exam. Exploding with rage, he beats the optometrist to death. The couple carries him out of the house, shoves him into his car, and pushes it into the lake. "Then it was in the papers. Mr. Willens found drowned," says Mrs. Quinn. "They said his head got bunged up knocking against the steering wheel. They said he was alive when he went in the water. What a laugh." The cleaning agents and paint she uses to wipe and cover up the mess in their home bring on her debilitating ailments. By the time she tells Enid all that happened, she is near death. After she dies, Enid must decide what to do with her knowledge of this grim chain of events.

*****

"The Love of a Good Woman" unfolds at a leisurely pace yet also flows with a breathless urgency—an understandable dynamic in a tale involving rape and murder but one that infuses the narrative arc of every story. Each delves into the turmoil of seemingly quotidian lives and the terrible things we do to one another, and to ourselves, often with an unwilled but inexorable forward momentum. In particular, Munro explores the lives of women: Kath and Sonje in "Jakarta" contending with polyamorous marriages. Eve in "Save the Reaper," who, in her sorrow and anxiety over a family situation, plays a game with her grandson that gets dangerously out of hand. The young woman in "Before the Change" who moves back home after her fiancé leaves her and discovers that her irascible father, a doctor, is an underground abortion provider. Pauline in "The Children Stay," who runs off with her lover, leaving her husband and young daughters behind. When her husband informs her that the children will stay with him, she tries to fathom what that will mean. "It was like a round cold stone in her gullet, like a cannonball. . . . This is acute pain. It will become chronic. Chronic means that it will be permanent but perhaps not constant. . . . And you'll learn some tricks to dull it or banish it."

Pauline's quiet acceptance of her pain resonates with that of the first-person narrator of "Cortes Island," a woman looking back on the first months of her marriage, when she and her husband lived in a basement flat with a busybody, Mrs. Gorrie, occupying the upper floors with her husband, a stroke victim confined to a wheelchair. At first, Mrs. Gorrie's intrusions upon the newlyweds seem fairly benign: forcing cookies on "the little bride" or inviting her up for tea when she would rather be alone in her basement trying her hand at creative writing. The situation devolves as the narrator discovers that Mrs. Gorrie has been letting herself into their apartment and rooting through their belongings—even their garbage, uncrumpling papers in the wastebasket and mocking the narrator's writing and revisions. "She isn't right in the head," Mrs. Gorrie says within earshot of the narrator. "She'd sit down there and say she's writing letters and she writes the same thing over and over again—it's not letters, it's the same thing over and over. She's not right in the head." The narrator grows anxious and fearful, but until she and her husband can move, she must put up with the abuse.

The scenario recalls Rachel Cusk's novel *Transit*, the second work in her *Outline* trilogy, whose main character, Faye, moves into a rundown home she proceeds to have renovated while the couple in the flat below persecutes her with their scorn, derision, and verbal abuse. They also spread lies about her to the other neighbors, sabotaging any chance Faye might have had of forging friendships after her messy divorce. Both *Transit* and "Cortes Island" probe the fears and anxieties surrounding neighbors, those whose proximity we have no choice but to accept, who seem to be—or truly are—prying, eavesdropping, judging.

At times throughout her story, the narrator of "Cortes Island" slips in comments about how life slipped out of her control, even after moving out from under Mrs. Gorrie's watchful eyes. Nor are men immune to the drag of routine and conventional social expectations. "Chess worked for a wholesale grocery firm," the narrator says of her husband. "He worked hard, not asking that the work he did fit in with any interests he might have had or have any purpose to it that he might once have honored. No purpose except to carry us both toward that life of lawnmowers and freezers which we believed we had no mind for. I might marvel at his submission, if I thought about it. His cheerful, you might say gallant, submission. But then, I thought, it's what men do." Women, too. Only rarely do people escape the soul-destroying nature of suburban married life, and if they do, they likely wind up like Pauline from "The Children Stay," mourning the loss of her daughters for a relationship that didn't last, after all.

I find the final story, "My Mother's Dream," the most compelling of all. It would do Samuel Beckett proud with its confounding narrative perspective, for the narrator recounts her own birth and the initial months of life, when she engaged in a fierce battle of wills with her mother. A posthumous child whose father was killed in the Second World War, she and her mother live with the deceased man's elderly mother and two middle-aged sisters. Not only does the narrator offer detailed accounts of experiences she could not possibly remember, but she also has access to the interiority of the women around her: her bewildered musician mother, who does not take to motherhood easily; her grandmother, sinking deeper into senility; her no-nonsense aunt Ailsa; and her emotionally fragile aunt Iona, the only one the narrator, as a baby, will tolerate.

All hell breaks loose when anyone other than Iona tries to touch her or talk to her, including her mother, whom she refers to by her first name, Jill. The chasm between them arises immediately, for as a newborn, the narrator "refused to take my mother's breast. I screamed blue murder. The big stiff breast might just as well have been a snouted beast rummaging in my face. Iona held me, she gave me a little warm boiled water, and I quieted down. . . . She knew herself to be the only person who didn't wince, who didn't feel the distant threat of annihilation, when I sent up my first signal wail." At just a few days old, the narrator seems to have calculated the best means of terrorizing everyone in the house: letting out deafening, high-pitched cries. Things worsen when Jill begins practicing her violin again. The sound of it sends the baby into a tailspin. That morning, the narrator says, "I woke without a whimper of discontent. No warning, no buildup. Just a shriek, a waterfall of shrieks descended on the house, a cry unlike any cry I'd managed before"—a cry throwing the household into an uproar until Jill goes outside to play and Iona runs to soothe the baby.

How has the narrator amassed all this information? It seems unlikely that Jill confided in her given the lifelong rift between them. The narrator-as-baby finally reconciles herself to being cared for by her mother—but with a twist. "I had to settle for Jill and for what I could get from her," she states, "even if it might look like half a loaf. To me it seems that it was only then that I became female. . . . I believe that it was only at the moment when I decided to come back, when I gave up the fight against my mother (which must have been a fight for something like her total surrender) and when in fact I chose survival over victory (death would have been victory), that I took on my female nature." What exactly does she mean? We "become female" only after resisting our mothers tooth and nail? Only when we begrudgingly accept their efforts to love and care for us? Or when we realize survival can only be had by emotionally walling them off? Throughout *The Love of a Good Woman*, characters resign themselves to unhappiness, estrangement, guilt, entrapment. The title story concludes with Enid envisioning a satisfying future with Mrs. Quinn's widower, but at a steep price.

*****

I can see why my mother read Alice Munro. They were of the same generation, their birthdays just three weeks apart in 1931. She would have appreciated the stories' cultural contexts, particularly concerning women. In "Jakarta," we learn Kath had to quit her job when her pregnancy began to show. The story also contains literary talk, which my mother would have enjoyed. Sonje reads Howard Fast because her husband tells her to. She and Kath discuss the male characters in Katherine Mansfield's story "At the Bay" and argue over concepts of love espoused in D.H. Lawrence's "The Fox." A man at a beach party recites lines from Matthew Arnold's "Dover Beach," a moving poem proffering love and fidelity as the only means of surviving a world that "Hath really neither joy, nor love, nor light, / Nor certitude, nor peace, nor help for pain." But the man in Munro's story quotes the poem to mock its ideas, not extol them: "'The sea of faith was once too at the full,'" he said humorously. "'And round earth's shore, lay like the folds of a bright girdle unfurled,'" an image reminding him of his former wife. Meanwhile, his current wife and mistress are also at the party, along with Kath, who carries on the quote from "Dover Beach" but stops when the man's wife emerges from the water—which doesn't stop the man from kissing Kath: "he waggled his cool tongue inside her mouth."

In "The Children Stay," after leaving her husband, Brian, Pauline considers the enormity of what she has done. "It was what a teacher at Brian's school had done, with the school secretary. He had run off with her. That was what it was called. Running off with. . . . It was spoken of disparagingly, humorously, enviously." My parents used similar language in recounting raucous stories of their faculty cohort in the 1960s and '70s. A priest had run off with a theology professor's wife. This person and that person were having an affair. So-and-so was always getting high. They would tell all of this to us kids when we were older, and we would laugh hysterically—easy to do when we didn't know any of the people, or the heartache, involved.

The passing of time. The cruelties of aging. Infidelity. Insecurities. Such is the stuff of Alice Munro's fictional landscape, and this essay barely scratches the surface of each beautifully wrought story. And yet, reading and writing about this book felt a bit like a chore. Like homework. Well, perhaps that's not the operative word. As someone who stayed in school, as student and then teacher, for as long as possible, I loved homework. I was the one in high school and college who finished papers days in advance of the deadline. While I read each story with interest and admire Munro's gifts, I'm not sure I can say I enjoyed reading these stories in June 2022. Perhaps the real world overshadowed the reading experience. Climate change, oil spills, police brutality, rising authoritarianism, nearly a million dead and counting from COVID-19 in the United States alone. And maniacs with access to assault rifles slaughtering children in their classrooms. Unbearable. Perhaps the gallery of characters in *The Love of a Good Woman* made their appearance at an inopportune time. Broken marriages, hateful neighbors, cruel or indifferent parents, and thankless children—I just didn't have the heart for it.

Chapter 9

When Everything Changed: The Amazing Journey of American Women from 1960 to the Present
by Gail Collins

Kristin,
This book is important. You all
need to know what the past—
during my lifetime—was like
and the hard work that
lies behind your privileges
today.
Love,
Mom

In one of my earliest childhood memories, I see my mother and several other women gathered around our dining room table. It's nighttime. The women talk and smoke. Stacks of letters and envelopes lie on the table along with notepads, pencils, and ashtrays. I'm not sure what's going on, but six-year-old me is impressed, for I can sense something important happening. Something urgent. And I feel proud because my mother is in charge, or so it seems. It's her house, after all. I come to learn that on that night and for many years, my mother worked tirelessly for the South Bend, Indiana, chapter of the League of Women Voters, serving as president for two years in the early 1970s. She was also on the board of the Indiana State League and a member of the Mayor's Committee on the Status of Women—all while raising three children and working outside the home ever since I, the youngest, started school. I thought about my mother while rereading *When Everything Changed: The Amazing Journey of American Women from 1960 to the Present*, by Gail Collins, which she gave me for Christmas in 2009 when I was 40 years old. She wrote a message inside: *Kristin, This book is important. You all need to know what the past—during my lifetime—was like and the hard work that lies behind your privileges today. Love, Mom.* My mother was 29 in 1960. As her inscription indicates, this is her story, and she needed me to know about it.

Collins explores women's roles, rights, and resistance to patriarchy from 1960, when women were relegated to the kitchen, to 2008, when Hillary Clinton ran for president. The book resounds with the voices of women who share personal experiences of oppression along with acts of defiance large and small that paved a more equitable way forward. Well into the 1970s, a woman still couldn't get a loan, a mortgage, or a credit card on her own, let alone a job with pay equal to that of a man. Throughout her book, Collins quotes one jaw-droppingly appalling comment about women after another from judges, businessmen, politicians, academics, film and television producers, advertisers, journalists, athletes, doctors, and scientists, including "a spokesman for NASA [who said] that any 'talk of an American spacewoman makes me sick to my stomach'"—a relentless onslaught of cruel, ignorant remarks reflecting a status quo that blighted women's lives.

I recall some of the sexist comments lobbed at me over the years. From the dentist in Chicago who, when I told him I was starting graduate school, became incensed that I didn't want to be a secretary for the rest of my life. From the dentist in Cincinnati who asked me how old I was (36) and if I had kids (no) and said, "Well, you better hurry up, missy!" From the professor who assumed I had moved to Cincinnati because of my husband's job and had enrolled in the English Ph.D. program just for something to do. It hadn't occurred to him that we had moved because of my professional aspirations. Then there was the older man seated next to me at a dinner party who asked me where I had gone to college. When I answered, "Notre Dame," he crossed his arms, gave me a steely look, and said, "You mean St. Mary's," the women's college across the road. He then proceeded to mock me for studying literature. I've had men (and one woman) tell me what a shame it is that Notre Dame began admitting women. And let's not forget the various men who've told me I'm selfish or lazy for not wanting children.

With every page of Collins's book, I considered my own feminist journey—and my feminist failures. Part I explores the year 1960, when "[t]he idea that men were supposed to be in charge went beyond conventional wisdom; it was regarded by many as scientific fact." Yet this "fact" had to be continually enforced by law and popular culture, for "by 1960 television was big business," Collins writes, "and if women were around at all, they were in the kitchen . . . When a script did turn its attention to the wife, daughter, or mother, it was frequently to remind her of her place and the importance of letting boys win." I appreciate Collins' acknowledgement at the start that her book reflects Western biases, and that women of low socioeconomic status and women of color often had no choice but to work outside the home, often in demeaning jobs for miserable pay. Mid-twentieth-century media, however, presented white middle-class suburbia as the norm, with the husband heading off to work in the morning and the wife spending her day doing housework in a dress, pearls, and heels. In fact, the "limited options for women who did work, and the postwar propaganda about the glories of homemaking, convinced the young women who were graduating from high school and college in the early 1960s that once you married, the good life was the stay-at-home life." For some, it was. Others felt buried alive.

Collins explores a common nuclear family dynamic of the time. "Men, in their capacity as breadwinners, were presumed to be the money managers on the home front as well as in business, and women were cut out of almost everything having to do with finances." Circumstances were different in my home growing up. In another childhood memory, my mother sits at the dining room table one night a month paying the bills, stacked in neat piles around her as she writes the checks. I don't think I ever saw my father write a check when I was a child. Mom paid the bills and doled out allowances. If my father needed cash, he went rifling through her wallet for it. I'm sure they made major financial decisions together, but in our house, she managed the day-to-day money.

I wish I could say the same for myself, but numbers and I don't get along. I bombed nearly every math class I ever took, passing by the skin of my teeth only because of one-on-one tutoring from our math professor neighbor across the street. In college, I begged the chair of the English Department to get me out of the university's math requirement. Math class meant frustration and tears. Even today, I can cheer myself up by reminding myself that I never have to take it again. My math trauma eventually served me well as an English professor when I encountered students who struggled with writing. While I couldn't relate to that particular problem, I could certainly empathize with students feeling anxious and hopeless when faced with a seemingly insurmountable academic task.

Years later, numbers continued to haunt me. Trying to pay bills and manage money on my own was a disaster. Words cannot express how grateful I am to have married a financially conscientious man who manages our money beautifully. We make all financial decisions together, we have joint accounts, and I have my own credit card to do with as I please, but he deals with the budget and bills, and I'm happy and relieved to have it so. Feminist fail. Yet when I talked about this with a woman from work years ago, she said she and her husband handled money the same way and that a bonus of marriage was having a partner who could deal with the finances. A friend from grad school whom I would certainly deem feminist cheerily informed me that she and her husband divvied up household chores along shamelessly retro gender lines: Cooking, cleaning, and laundry for her. Yard work, home repair, and taking out the trash for him.

Reflecting on such arrangements, I'm reminded of Roxane Gay's exploration in *Bad Feminist* of the tension between "essential feminism"—"the notion that there are right and wrong ways to be a feminist and that there are consequences for doing feminism wrong"—and "the complexities of human experience. There seems to be little room" in essential feminism, she writes, "for multiple or discordant points of view." In the book's concluding essay, Gay enumerates all the ways she's "doing feminism wrong": her favorite color is pink, she reads *Vogue* unironically, she doesn't know anything about cars, and she fantasizes about "hav[ing] a closet full of pretty shoes and purses and matching outfits"—all while "remain[ing] deeply committed to the issues important to the feminist movement." I'm grateful for Gay's honesty in sharing what are also my concerns regarding feminist integrity. Maybe I shouldn't feel so bad about my math phobia, after all. Or maybe I should take Finance 101.

Along with women's struggles to earn fair wages and wield autonomy over their money, Collins addresses the fraught subject of clothing, specifically "pants, so comfortable and so freighted with symbolism." After briefly rehearsing the history of women's clothing, which "seemed to have been designed to make it difficult to move, let alone get any work done," she discusses women's clothing more recently along with official and unofficial dress codes dictating women's attire at home, at work, and on the athletic field. In fact, the introduction to *When Everything Changed* opens with the story of Lois Rabinowitz, a young secretary who "unwittingly became the feature story of the day in New York City when she went down to traffic court to pay her boss's speeding ticket" wearing pants. It was the summer of 1960. The magistrate "exploded in outrage" and ordered her to go home and change. "Instead, the secretary gave the ticket to her husband" so he could pay the fine. The magistrate reprimanded the husband and told him he better get his wife in line. Collins also writes of "when Ruth Bader Ginsburg applied for a Supreme Court clerkship [in 1963] and Justice Felix Frankfurter rejected her after asking, 'Does she wear skirts? I can't stand girls in pants.'"

As Placement Director at the Notre Dame Law School, my mother wore a skirt, pantyhose, and low heels to work each day. She loathed pantyhose and complained about them constantly—how uncomfortable they were, not to mention expensive. She looked forward to many things when she retired at age 60—sleeping in, traveling, doing whatever she wanted with her day, but most of all, never putting on another pair of hose. As a child, I thought of pantyhose as a rite of passage into adulthood. My friends and I would wear our mothers' hose while playing dress-up, the excess nylon bunching up around our ankles and knees. I remember the plastic L'eggs containers that looked like eggs and the pink plastic pouches the No Nonsense brand came in. Not yet forced to wear them, I thought they were fun. I would come to know better.

For a couple of years in the early 1990s, soon after college, I worked as a secretary at an upscale hotel in downtown Chicago. All female staff had to wear a skirt or dress. No pants, even though we secretaries were never seen by hotel guests. In fact, staff were not permitted in the lobby or anywhere guests might see us. One day after work, I had an ingrown toenail removed. It must have been bad, because while I didn't watch the procedure (they gave me a magazine to hold in front of my face so I wouldn't be tempted to look), the podiatrist's assistant kept saying, "Oh, God!" I went home with crutches and a giant bandage around my big toe. It was the dead of winter, with piles of snow on the ground, and I didn't want to deal with a skirt and tights while dressing for work the next day. How could I force a bandaged big toe into a pair of tights? I called the hotel in the morning and spoke to one of the managers, explaining the situation and asking if I could, just this once, wear pants and boots to work. The female manager said no. I wore pants, anyway.

Not long after our mother died, my sister told me "The Story of the Green Pantsuit." One night in the early 1970s, my mother wore a green pantsuit to a faculty party, apparently a bold move for the time. And apparently, my father was mortified. He kept several steps ahead of her throughout the evening, and at the end of the night said to her, "It's okay. I don't think anyone noticed." She never told me this story, but my sister remembers hearing it from her several times, so it must have stuck in her craw. Given '70s fashion, it could well have been an abominable pantsuit. I wonder what shade of green it was. Avocado? Olive? Lime? Army? I realize that's not the point. I suppose I'm just trying to spin it so my father doesn't come across quite so badly. This was not one of his finer moments.

Collins spoke with women around the country who shared memories of their mothers' awakening feminist consciousness. Many recalled the day Betty Friedan's 1963 bombshell, *The Feminine Mystique*, entered their homes. "Anna Quindlen, the novelist and columnist, says she remembers few specific details from her childhood, but one of the most vivid is seeing her mother 'hunched over this paperback, frowning, twin divots between her dark brows.'" I, too, remember seeing a worn paperback of *The Feminine Mystique* in our house, compiled from information Friedan had gathered from thousands of women "slowly going crazy in their well-appointed homes." According to Friedan, there were no "'happy housewives'—or scant few. Women were being forced to waste their lives on meaningless household chores in order to create profits for manufacturers of household goods," Collins writes. "They were being duped into believing homemaking was their natural destiny by gushy, unrealistic articles in women's magazines—all edited by men." I can see *The Feminine*

Mystique clear as day on a shelf in the basement of my parents' next home, too, built after I graduated from college. My mother pointed it out to me long before that, though, and pressed it into my hands several times over the years. I honestly cannot remember if I read it. If so, I guess it didn't make much of an impression. If not, I don't know why I resisted.

I remember the term "MCP" bandied about by my mother when I was little—when she listened to the news or talked with her friends. "It stands for male chauvinist pig," she told me, and I began parroting her upon getting a taste of it. One day after a heavy snowfall, I followed my father and brother as they headed out for a walk. I wanted to go with them, but they sent me back home, saying I wouldn't be able to keep up. I was eight. I went back inside, kicked off my boots, and began to cry. My mother was in the kitchen and came over to comfort me. I'm pretty sure she muttered the word "sexist." Of course, at eight years old, I *wouldn't* have been able to keep up with my brother, twelve, and my father through more than a foot of snow. I would have quickly grown tired and slowed them down. It wasn't my gender but my age that was the issue. Or so I think. I'm not sure how to parse such long-ago moments.

My mother's feminist example took root early on, but my father made an impression as well. Both of my parents valued education, read *The New York Times* and the *New Yorker*, watched *PBS Newshour*, and encouraged us in all our endeavors—academics, sports, music, or dance. I always did well in school. I never felt cowed by male classmates or teachers, and throughout grade school and high school, I had women teachers I liked and respected. I played sports as soon as I was old enough and up through my senior year of high school. I was always fairly outspoken, and as a white person from a middle-class household, I took it for granted that I could be whatever I wanted when I grew up.

But when it comes down to it, I didn't have a very profound grasp of feminism or feminist consciousness until grad school in my late twenties/early thirties, when I read Eve Kosofsky Sedgwick, Adrienne Rich, Audre Lorde, Jane Marcus, Alice Walker, Nancy Chodorow, Paula Gunn Allen, Gloria Anzaldúa, Ana Castillo, Patricia Hill Collins, and Carolyn Heilbrun, among many others, along with Virginia Woolf's *A Room of One's Own* and *Three Guineas*—books and writers and ideas that cracked my brain wide open. I felt a strong, instant pull towards such material and spent the next two decades deeply engaged in feminist theory in my research, writing, and teaching.

But oh, what must my mother—and father—have thought of me during my middle school years? When I got my hands on some sort of orangey face powder and patted it on one morning before school when I was in the fourth grade. My mother said, "Absolutely not," and made me wash it off. When my friends and I obsessed over clothing and swapped outfits in the girls' bathroom the minute we got to school. The sweaters, pants, shirts, and skirts would pile up into a soft, colorful mountain. When I slept with pink foam curlers in my hair. I once brought my father to desperate tears over my insistence on wearing a Bonnie Bell Lip Smacker as a necklace. Other times, my parents relaxed and rolled with it. I suppose this was just ordinary girlhood in middle America.

It was certainly ordinary to have Barbie dolls. Any mention of them in Collins's book made me smile—and cringe. "The first Barbie dolls appeared in American toy stores in 1959," she writes, "and they were a revelation. Dolls had always been shaped more or less like little girls, with a firm, stocky, and undefined body. But Barbie was *built*." I had several Barbies, plus a Ken doll, that I played with constantly. I had the Barbie convertible, camping set, airplane, and townhouse—my big-ticket Christmas gift when I was eight years old. I didn't have the swimming pool but made do with the bathroom sink. My friend Mia had the Barbie penthouse—so glamorous. I was always buying new outfits for my Barbies, and my friend Cece and I made clothes for them on our mothers' sewing machines.

Later, as a grad student and new instructor, I raged against Barbie. The dictum was that if an actual woman had Barbie's proportions and high-heeled feet, she would topple over. I marveled that my mother let me have Barbies, wholly incompatible, I believed, with feminist principles—although my sister recalls that we were only allowed to acquire them second-hand. Collins writes of parents who banned Barbie from the house when their daughters were young, and she notes Barbie's "midlife crisis in 1999 when she was challenged by the Bratz dolls," clad in "miniskirts, midriff-bearing tops, fishnet stockings, and feather boas"—dolls even more sexualized than Barbie.

Along with my younger self's devotion to Barbie, I reflect on other choices I've made. I took my husband's name when we married in 1995, arguing that since his and my father's surnames were both patronyms, there really wasn't much of a difference. Yet there's a paper trail displaying my wavering thoughts on the matter. My college diploma says Kristin Elizabeth Kommers, my master's diploma says Kristin Elizabeth Czarnecki, and my Ph.D. diploma says Kristin Kommers Czarnecki. My husband jokingly called me Kristin Cougar Mellencamp. It turns out I wasn't alone, though. In the 1990s, "young women freely referred to themselves as 'Ms.,' [but] they were more likely to take their husbands' names after they married than their older sisters had been." Was I complicit in the '90s backlash against "old-school" feminist rhetoric and activism? The situation "was, in one way, exactly what the elders had been hoping for—American women who had grown up confident that they were entitled to all the educational and career opportunities that boys got," Collins writes. "But there was also the disappointment of realizing that the younger women took it all for granted." I guess I did, too.

Collins speaks with "the writer Jane O'Reilly," who "recalled that [as a housewife in the 1960s] she had 'never earned my own living, never taken a trip alone, never taken total responsibility for a single decision.'" I have done all these things as a matter of course and often lost sight of how such ordinary actions were out of women's reach for so long. I wasn't especially political in early adulthood and sometimes declined to vote. I was a sucker for Clinique Bonus Time. I began dyeing my hair when I was just 26, believing the rich auburn color I inherited from my mother was starting to look dingy. Then I was trapped. I've spent untold hours and obscene amounts of money at salons ever since. I shave my legs and armpits. I stay thin. Am I performing femininity according to outdated, sexist standards? Am I a disgrace to my feminist foremothers?

Yet such misgivings risk buying into tired old stereotypes about feminists—stereotypes Mary Wollstonecraft handily dispatched in 1792 in *A Vindication of the Rights of Woman* but that continue to rear their heads. "The sense that feminists were all homely had dogged every struggle for women's rights in American history," Collins states, quoting Betty Friedan on the subject: "I did not agree with the message some were trying to push—that to be a liberated woman you had to make yourself ugly, to stop shaving under your arms, to stop wearing makeup or pretty dresses or any skirts at all." When Gloria Steinem came on the scene, men used her extraordinary good looks to deny her feminist bona fides. Such criticism never ceased. "The part that's hurtful is that having worked hard and continuing to work hard at 73, I still find accomplishments attributed to my appearance," Steinem once said. "I would have thought I could outgrow that by now." On the contrary, it's the culture at large that has some maturing to do.

I've tried to do better as well. A few years ago, I got swept up in the excitement surrounding the centennial anniversary of the Nineteenth Amendment. I watched *Iron Jawed Angels*, the 2004 film based on the work of Alice Paul, Lucy Burns, and the generation of suffragists who fought for women's right to vote. Days later, I showed the film on campus to a group of freshman women. Galvanized and eager for more, I read *The Woman's Hour: The Great Fight to Win the Vote*, by Elaine Weiss; *Suffrage: Women's Long Battle for the Vote*, by Ellen Carol Dubois; *Votes for Women: A Portrait of Persistence*, Kate Clarke Lemay's beautifully illustrated volume; and *Vanguard: How Black Women Broke Barriers, Won the Vote, and Insisted on Equality for All*, by Martha S. Jones. I am indebted to these writers, heroes, and women everywhere who worked hard and sacrificed for the freedoms I have always enjoyed.

Unfortunately, Collins writes, "for the most part, the generation [in the 1960s and '70s] that took the risks, filed the suits, held the press conferences, and made the demands were not the ones who benefited." When they did, it was often at the expense of other women. "Madeleine Kunin, whose political career had begun to get some traction, realized very fast that it was her babysitter that made her work possible. . . . 'One of the ironies of the women's movement is that women like me obtained our liberty because of other women who agreed to help us as our housekeepers, babysitters, and cleaning women.'" Sara Ahmed writes powerfully about this issue in *Living a Feminist Life*, arguing that we remain complicit in women's oppression when we dump the most burdensome, monotonous, underpaid labor on other women.

"Feminism needs to refuse this division of labor, this freeing up of time and energy for some by the employment of the limbs of others," Ahmed states. "A feminist army that gives life and vitality to some women's arms by taking life and vitality from other women's arms is reproducing inequality and injustice. That is not freedom." In her final chapter, Collins reflects on the related and ongoing conundrum of women trying to balance work and family. "The feminist movement of the late twentieth century created a new United States in which women ran for president, fought for their country, argued before the Supreme Court, performed heart surgery, directed movies, and flew into space," she writes. "But it did not resolve the tension of trying to raise children and hold down a job at the same time." The fault lies not with the feminist movement, however, but with the refusal of those in power—government representatives, titans of industry—to ratify meaningful change, such as universal health care, paid maternity/paternity leave, and subsidized childcare.

What can we do as individuals? Am I living a feminist life? I taught women's literature almost exclusively in my eighteen years as an English professor. I wrote and published literary criticism exploring women, gender, anti-patriarchal ideology, and decolonization. For two years, I was the faculty co-advisor for the Student Women and Gender Society and organized several Take Back the Night events on campus. I planned a one-day symposium on sexual assault awareness and prevention in which students, staff, and faculty shared personal stories, presented research, exhibited art, and held roundtable discussions. For two and a half years, I served on the Board of Directors of the Bluegrass Rape Crisis Center (now the Ampersand Sexual Violence Resource Center). And I still get highlights, shave my legs, and am happy for my husband to take care of the bills. Are these irreconcilable contradictions? I don't know. I do know that humans are ever-changing, that we exist on a continuum, and that feminism will continue to shape my life in new and unforeseen ways. Having left academia, I look forward to exploring other avenues for feminist expression and activism.

I began this essay on June 24, 2022, the day the Supreme Court overturned *Roe v. Wade*. Since then, I have vacillated between fury and sorrow while doom-scrolling through Twitter, reading the newspapers, and communicating in lengthy text chains with my feminist sisters—brilliant, creative, strong women friends from every stage of my life. We all experienced whiplash, going from euphoria over the 50th anniversary of Title IX to grief over the end of the constitutional right to an abortion. We vow never to give up the fight for reproductive justice. We support women writers, artists, and activists. And we work with our fear, sadness, and rage to confront misogyny in our society. How I wish I could talk to my mother about all of this. Instead, I wear her ERA bracelet from back in the day, one of my most treasured possessions, and strive to channel her fighting spirit.

Chapter 10

A Good Man is Hard to Find and Other Stories
by Flannery O'Connor

Kristin:
F. O'Connor and Thomas Merton are
two authors who have
influenced me greatly.
Hope they do the same
for you.
Love
Dad
A Merry Xmas 2006

Mid-summer, I had a long, lovely dream about my dad. In it, he was middle-aged and healthy and wore a dark blue windbreaker. He had a jacket for every ten-degree variation in the weather, it seemed. In the dream, we were spending a wonderful day together on Notre Dame's campus. It was good to see him and be with him, if only for a few hours while I slept, and if only in profile, for it occurred to me upon waking that when he appears in my dreams, I usually see him from behind or from the side, not full-on. I guess that's my dream-brain's way of acknowledging that he's really gone.

The next morning, I perused my bookshelves for the umpteenth time to see if there were any other books I could do without—any others I could donate to the local library beyond the hundred or so I had already culled as my husband and I prepared to downsize from a house to an apartment in our move to Gloucester, Massachusetts. The first thing we did when we moved into our house in Georgetown, Kentucky, fourteen years previously, was hire a carpenter to build floor-to-ceiling bookshelves along one wall of the dining room. The carpenter also built shelf inserts to hold our CDs—over a thousand of them. We were losing all that shelf space in the move, so I had to get real about what I was actually going to read or reread.

So on a Sunday morning as our moving date approached, the dream about my dad from the night before still vivid in my mind, I went over to the shelves yet again to see what else could go. Adichie, Alvarez, Carson, Cisneros, Groff, Harjo, Joyce, Kingston, Lahiri, Morrison. It was like having to choose a friend to never see again or deciding which pet to take back to the shelter. Impossible, but I had to be ruthless. When I got to the Os, I pulled Flannery O'Connor's *A Good Man is Hard to Find and Other Stories* from the shelf, thinking it was redundant because we also have *The Complete Stories*. Then I opened it and saw my dad's inscription, and my heart skipped a beat. I had been wondering what to read next for this project, and here it was. My father had led me right to it.

I hadn't read Flannery O'Connor in decades, but indelible images and lines from her stories instantly sprang to mind: the hapless grandmother in "A Good Man is Hard to Find." The ferocious Hazel Motes of *Wise Blood*. That horrendous and immortal line from "Revelation": "Go back to hell where you came from, you old wart hog." I read "Revelation" and several other O'Connor stories in my senior seminar, Southern Renaissance, as an English major at Notre Dame. O'Connor was not only a southern writer but also a gothic writer, and above all, as far as my father was concerned, a Catholic writer. As I got ready to read the book, I determined to focus on the Catholic aspect of things to understand its allure for my dad as I couldn't square these strange, darkly funny stories with my father or my own experience of Catholicism.

Before doing so, though, I needed to contend with O'Connor's racism. I don't know whether my father read her in real time, while she was publishing her fiction in the 1950s and early '60s, or later in life, or both, but he apparently opened her books and thought, *Catholic*. As a reader in 2022, I open her book and think, *Yikes!* The n-word is everywhere: in narrative exposition, in dialogue, even in a story title. Every time I come across it, I wince. O'Connor was born and raised in Georgia, only living away from home while earning her M.F.A. at the Iowa Writers Workshop and staying with friends in New York City for a few months after that. By all accounts, she wanted to spread her wings much farther than Milledgeville, Georgia, but her lupus diagnosis at age 25 meant she had to go home, where she lived with her mother, sought treatment for her disease, and settled in to write. The n-word was all around her—in the air she breathed and the water she drank, emblematic of racism both casual and deadly proliferating in the United States at the time, especially in the South.

I know that O'Connor sometimes used the n-word ironically in her fiction, or put it in the mouth of a detestable character, or employed it to depict the social fabric of mid-twentieth-century middle Georgia. That doesn't make it any easier to read, however, or negate the fact that she also used the word in her personal correspondence. Then there's her infamous refusal to entertain James Baldwin in Georgia. "No I can't see James Baldwin in Georgia," she wrote to her friend Maryat Lee. "It would cause the greatest trouble and disturbance and disunion. In New York it would be nice to meet him; here it would not. I observe the traditions of the society I feed on—it's only fair. Might as well expect a mule to fly as me to see James Baldwin in Georgia. I have read one of his stories and it was a good one."

In her biography of O'Connor (also a gift from my father), Jean W. Cash doesn't shy away from her subject's problematic writings on race, but she reminds us to keep them in context. "If certain of her characters . . . spout racist garbage," Cash writes, "they do so because they are realistic representatives of the Deep South mentality that O'Connor so carefully depicted." Regarding her disparaging remarks about African Americans in letters to friends, Cash argues that O'Connor was being mischievous—that she enjoyed entertaining her friends in her letters and knew precisely how to push their buttons. Cash cites O'Connor's correspondence with Maryat Lee in particular. "As the Civil Rights movement gained momentum . . . and Maryat Lee became personally involved in it, O'Connor enjoyed portraying herself as a racial conservative against Lee as Civil Rights activist."

Recent essays on O'Connor and race focus less on her fiction and more on personal writings only recently made available to scholars. In his June 2020 *New Yorker* article, "How Racist Was Flannery O'Connor?" Paul Elie cites the letters and postcards eighteen-year-old O'Connor wrote while on a trip up North that "show [her] as a bigoted young woman." He acknowledges that it's "not fair to judge a writer by her juvenilia. But, as she developed into a keenly self-aware writer, the habit of bigotry persisted in her letters," and "O'Connor lovers have been downplaying [it] ever since." His article responds in large part to Angela Alaimo O'Donnell's book *Radical Ambivalence: Race in Flannery O'Connor*. "Although [the author] is palpably anguished about O'Connor's race problem," Elie writes, she errs in "treating O'Connor as 'transgressive in her writing about race' but prone to lapses and excesses that stemmed from social forces beyond her control." Elie urges O'Connor scholars not to "sidestep" the "racist passages" in her writings but to "face them squarely" and treat her and her works "with the seriousness that a great writer deserves."

O'Donnell's rejoinder to Elie appears in the August 2020 issue of *Commonweal*. In "The 'Canceling' of O'Connor? It Never Should Have Happened," O'Donnell recounts, and rues, Loyola University Maryland's decision in the summer of 2020 to "remove Flannery O'Connor's name from one of its buildings"—a decision likely stemming, O'Donnell believes, from Elie's *New Yorker* piece—from its "incendiary title" to its misrepresentation of her book, whose purpose, O'Donnell explains, was "to arrive at an understanding of how a writer who created the powerful anti-racist parables we all know and admire—'Everything That Rises Must Converge,' 'The Artificial N*****' (my asterisks), 'Judgment Day,' 'Revelation,' and more—was in her personal correspondence also capable of entertaining and confessing racist thoughts." Readers of William Faulkner confront the same dilemma, which Casey Cep addresses in her November 2020 *New Yorker* piece, "William Faulkner's Demons." Such discussions remind me of teaching Joseph Conrad's *Heart of Darkness*, which seesaws between dehumanizing the Africans on the one hand and expressing empathy for them on the other, including condemning the colonial atrocities perpetrated upon them. Is it Conrad's voice we're hearing or his character Marlow's? Where do we draw the line between them? To what extent do they converge?

"Elie's [*New Yorker* piece] has caused a great deal of damage," O'Donnell claims. "As soon as it was released online, Twitter lit up with public denunciations of O'Connor and avowals from former admirers that they would never read—or teach—her books again." Soon, a student-led petition at Loyola to remove her name from the building garnered over 1,000 signatures. "Many of the signers admitted to not knowing who O'Connor was, but they heartily affirmed her erasure," O'Donnell states, and she feels it incumbent upon her to "intervene in the cancelation of Flannery O'Connor." Instead of canceling certain authors and their works, could we try to establish a fruitful discourse around them?

I used to tell my students that for me, the more interesting question is not, "Was O'Connor (or Faulkner or Conrad) a racist," but, "What can these writings tell us about concepts of race, racial issues, and race relations of the time? And how might we take what we learn and pave a more equitable path forward?" Of course, that's easy for me, a white woman, to say. O'Donnell believes that "The voices of artists who offer a perspective that seems out of step with our moment are often the very people we should be hearkening to." Yet O'Connor's use of the n-word and comments on race don't *seem* "out of step with our moment." They *are* out of step. And what of the violence and trauma endured by African Americans because of racism and the n-word? I wonder what sort of conversations my dad and I might have had about the subject, and I chalk it up to another opportunity lost. I then forge ahead with *A Good Man is Hard to Find and Other Stories*.

*****

Reading the explosive title story feels like being shoved onto a runaway train careening into O'Connor country. There they are again, the family setting out on a weekend's excursion only to be murdered in cold blood by an escaped convict, The Misfit, and his cronies. The grandmother, terrified and feeling guilty for causing the car accident that attracted the criminals' attention, tries to reason with The Misfit as he holds forth about crime and punishment, and how our path in life hinges on our belief in Jesus Christ. "'If He did what He said, then it's nothing for you to do but thow [*sic*] away everything and follow Him," he says, "and if He didn't, then it's nothing for you to do but enjoy the few minutes you got left the best way you can—by killing somebody or burning down his house or doing some other meanness to him. No pleasure but meanness,' he said, and his voice had become almost a snarl." The Misfit is the first of several would-be philosophers in the stories, like Tom Shiftlet in "The Life You Save May Be Your Own" or the conman in "Good Country People." What's unnerving is that their twisted logic often rings true.

"A Good Man is Hard to Find" brings Alice Munro's "Save the Reaper" to mind, although Eve, the grandmother in Munro's story, manages to avert disaster after her ill-advised car ride with her grandchildren. At least, she averts it for the time being, for the story hints that the hitchhiker she picked up may return to harm the family. As the story ends, though, they're safe, unlike O'Connor's doomed characters. "A Good Man" becomes excruciating as The Misfit's henchmen shepherd the family members into the woods. Five pistol shots ring out. The father and son are killed first. Moments later, the mother, daughter, and baby. Pointless murders wiping out three generations when, at the end, The Misfit shoots the grandmother three times in the chest.

My heart aches for the boy in the next story, "The River," whose parents farm him out to various babysitters so they can party in their apartment. Four years old, he's inured to neglect, disappointment, and humiliation. When a babysitter takes him to a river to be baptized, the boy seems startled but not transformed after his plunge into the water. He "was too shocked to cry. . . 'Don't forget his mamma,' Mrs. Connin," the babysitter, "called. 'He wants you to pray for his mamma. She's sick.' . . . 'Is she in pain?'" the preacher asks. "The child stared at him. 'She hasn't got up yet,' he said in a high dazed voice. 'She has a hangover.'" When he wakes the next morning, he realizes there may be more to life than empty cupboards and overflowing ashtrays, and he makes his way back to the river. "He intended not to fool with preachers anymore but to Baptize himself and to keep on going this time until he found the Kingdom of Christ in the river. He put his head under the water and pushed forward." After several aborted attempts to sink, the river's current grabs him, and "since he was moving quickly and knew that he was getting somewhere, all his fury and his fear left him." What is there to say when a four-year-old prefers oblivion to his reality?

I love the first, sinister sentence of "The Life You Save May Be Your Own," which harbors an entire story in and of itself: "The old woman and her daughter were sitting on their porch when Mr. Shiftlet came up their road for the first time." What we have here is a hustler—a shifty character who's chosen his prey carefully and who won't relent until he has what he wants. On this first day, he joins the women on the porch and matter-of-factly tells them he may be a liar. He, too, is a dime store philosopher. "There's one of these doctors in Atlanta that's taken a knife and cut the human heart—the human heart . . . out of a man's chest and held it in his hand," he says, "and studied it like it was a day-old chicken, and lady . . . he don't know no more about it than you or me."

He's after the woman's money and property, of course, especially the automobile in her barn. She knows it but urges him to marry her deaf nonverbal daughter, anyway, which he does in an elaborate ruse to make off with the old woman's money and car. After abandoning the daughter in a diner and getting cussed out by a young hitchhiker, "Mr. Shiftlet felt that the rottenness of the world was about to engulf him. He raised his [lone] arm and let it fall again to his breast. 'Oh Lord!' he prayed. 'Break forth and wash the slime from this earth!' . . . Very quickly he stepped on the gas and with his stump sticking out the window he raced the galloping shower into Mobile." Does he consider himself part of the slime? Or does he think he's above it and that somewhere up the road exists a space free of abysmal encounters with other human beings?

Time and again, O'Connor's stories expose our vulnerability—to mischief and lies. To manipulation. To the annihilation of all we thought we knew. And to anyone who decides to saunter up the road, sit themself down, and refuse to budge. We are powerless against such intrusions, illustrated to supreme effect in "A Circle of Fire" as three boys walk onto Mrs. Cope's farm, setting an ominous tone that never lets up. One of them tells her his father used to work on the farm, which is how they knew to seek it out. What do they want, these taciturn boys? "You keep out of their way," Mrs. Cope tells her young daughter. "'They'll be gone in the morning.' But in the morning they were not gone." Of course they weren't, and Mrs. Cope cannot cope despite her convictions in her own authority and righteousness. The nosy, cynical hired help, however, pegs the situation exactly: "'There ain't a thing you can do about it,' Mrs. Pritchard said."

The boys' hostility towards Mrs. Cope burns as hotly as the dry brush they set on fire in her woods. As she, her daughter, and her farmhands watch the smoke rise into the sky, her daughter hears "wild high shrieks of joy as if the prophets were dancing in the fiery furnace, in the circle the angel had cleared for them." Prophets tormenting a woman, committing crimes? Angels aiding and abetting them? Transformation can only happen via destruction, the story proclaims, a violent burning away of the old to make way for the new. But what exactly is the new? And if the boys are prophets, what does that make Mrs. Cope? Is she akin to the grandmother in "A Good Man is Hard to Find" in that her only means of salvation lies in her ruin? After finishing "A Circle in the Fire," I wrote "apocalyptic Catholicism" in my notes and then learned that such a term actually exists.

In her article on contemporary apocalyptic Catholicism, Amy Luebbers interviews "believers" who identify "political evil" as the "dissolution of a sacred society," which seems to tally with the stance emerging from O'Connor's stories on the sacred and the secular. The publisher's blurb on the back cover of my book cites O'Connor's "stated purpose" as "to reveal the mystery of God's grace in everyday life." In her biography, Cash similarly states that O'Connor "used her talent—her extraordinary genius as a writer—not for self-aggrandizement but to lead other would-be Christians toward transcendent grace." Thus the "pivotal—and ambivalent—struggle toward Grace" in her first novel, *Wise Blood*, "became the central concern of most of her fiction." Characters throughout *A Good Man is Hard to Find and Other Stories* sense, or yearn for, or find themselves on the cusp of grace, even—perhaps especially—the most troubled, deviant, or violent. O'Connor's secular characters, on the other hand, cannot—or will not—let grace into their lives.

Mrs. McIntyre in "The Displaced Person" is one such secularist, deliberating over whether to fire the Polish refugee in her employ, Mr. Guizac, and deflecting any moral or ethical qualms about doing so. She confronts a foil in Father Flynn, the priest who had convinced her to harbor the Guizac family in the first place. In his visits to the farm to see how they're getting on, Father Flynn expresses more interest in the peacock on the property, especially its magnificent tail. On one such visit, the priest looks over at the birds:

> The cock stopped suddenly and curving his neck backwards, he raised his tail and spread it with a shimmering timbrous noise. Tiers of small pregnant suns floated in a green-gold haze over his head. The priest stood transfixed, his jaw slack. Mrs. McIntyre wondered where she had ever seen such an idiotic old man. "Christ will come like that!" he said in a loud gay voice . . . Mrs. McIntyre's face assumed a set puritanical expression and she reddened. Christ in the conversation embarrassed her the way sex had her mother.

As Cash notes, peacocks in O'Connor's stories symbolize transcendence, spiritual insight, or the presence of God. Early in "The Displaced Person," the peacock's tail appears "glittering green-gold and blue in the sunlight . . . It flowed out on either side like a floating train and his head on the long blue reed-like neck was drawn back as if his attention were fixed in the distance on something no one else could see," especially not Mrs. McIntyre, oblivious to the grace in her midst. She cannot bring herself to fire Mr. Guizac, however, and after he dies in a tractor accident, she becomes gravely ill, her only visitor Father Flynn, who came each week to "sit by the side of her bed and explain the doctrines of the Church." Is her condition psychosomatic, brought on by a guilty conscience? Is she being punished for her callous treatment of her workers and for her secularism? What does O'Connor mean to say about post-war America as she ends the story with Mrs. McIntyre captive to the priest she distrusts and dislikes?

Catholic apocalypticists are also cultural fundamentalists, Luebbers explains, who espouse extremely conservative social norms. "To these believers, The End is the means by which the sacred will be reestablished in the world." Those she interviewed "view the 'freedom' of abortion in the United States as the primary reason for the coming Tribulation," for instance. Believers also "express a desire for political authority, but only of the type supportive of pro-family social nucleus and traditionally-bound, regulated liberties." While a "traditional value system underlying social and religious beliefs is not isolated to apocalypticists," Luebbers explains, "these believers indicate that a conversion experience served as a mechanism of transition that enforced these beliefs religiously while providing grounding for their mystical, apocalyptic perspective."

I find such a perspective disturbing and hard to fathom. I doubt that O'Connor could be deemed a Catholic apocalypticist, though, or a cultural fundamentalist—she who defied the gender and social norms of her time in leaving home (until her lupus diagnosis) and becoming a professional writer. Cash explains that as O'Connor "often asserted, her major impetus for writing was to undercut the secularity of her era, to guide the unbelieving toward belief; in addition, she was totally dedicated to the rules of Roman Catholicism." She attended Mass nearly every day of her life, "complied with dietary restrictions imposed by her faith, and read theology with considerable enthusiasm." She asked her priest's permission to read works in the Catholic Index of Forbidden Books, and in a 1955 letter to her friend Betty Hester, she identifies the Eucharist as "the center of existence for me; all the rest of life is expendable." We see such expendability in the stories.

In "A Good Man is Hard to Find," the grandmother's moment of selflessness hastens her murder, for when The Misfit laments his life's trajectory and his exclusion from the Kingdom of God, she expresses true compassion when up to that point, she had spoken to try to placate him and save her own skin. "'Listen,' she said, 'you shouldn't call yourself The Misfit because I know you're a good man at heart. I can just look at you and tell.'" When she encourages him to pray, he tells her how he had felt buried alive in prison, and about his bewilderment and outrage at suffering a punishment incommensurate with his crime, as he sees it. "I wisht I had of been there" in the time of Jesus, he says. "It ain't right I wasn't there because if I had of been there I would of known" if Jesus actually did the things he said. "I would of known and I wouldn't be like I am now." Suddenly, "the grandmother's head cleared for an instant . . . and she murmured, 'Why you're one of my babies. You're one of my own children!'"

When she touches his shoulder, he "sprang back as if a snake had bitten him and shot her three times through the chest. . . . 'She would of been a good woman,' The Misfit said, 'if it had been somebody there to shoot her every minute of her life'"—if she had been jolted by crisis into sincere expressions of Christian love and charity.

O'Connor's devotion to Catholicism resonates in terms of my father, who also had deep respect for the "rules of Roman Catholicism." Her comment on the Eucharist sparks one memory in particular. On vacation with my parents in Rockport, Massachusetts, some years ago, we went out to brunch one Sunday. No doubt my father had gone to Mass that morning, while my mother and I stayed home. I don't know how the conversation at brunch got started or what it was about, exactly, but at one point, my dad practically shouted, "The Eucharist is the most important part of the Mass!" People at other tables turned to look at us, he said it so loudly. He sounded angry, probably because I wasn't expressing interest in the topic.

Like O'Connor, I was born into Catholicism, as she often said of herself. Our family went to Mass every Sunday and several times during Holy Week. I went to Sunday school for a few years when I was little, and when I was in the third grade, the Sunday school teachers gave me a prize for asking the best questions. Was I a skeptic? At the very least, I must have wanted various ideas explained more fully, portending, maybe, my future as an academic. I wonder about the quality of those classes, though. At dinner one night when I was eight or nine years old, I asked my father what the difference was between Catholicism and Christianity. He got this look on his face, and my brother said, "That's how good our Sunday school classes are." I vaguely remember my first communion, and I vividly remember taking classes to prepare for my Confirmation. Years later, my husband and I went through Pre-Cana, the required course a couple must take in order to have a Catholic wedding. There were months-long Pre-Cana programs, but we found one in Chicago, where we were living at the time, that could be completed in one afternoon. These days, Pre-Cana classes can be taken online.

All this is to say, I guess I was fairly immersed in Catholicism growing up, but it never fully took hold. I went to Mass dutifully, but it didn't entice or excite me. I attended Mass off and on as an adult more for the chance to sit in peace and quiet for an hour than to fulfill a sacred obligation. Eventually, though, my husband and I stopped going to Mass and disavowed Catholicism, appalled by the Catholic Church's long history of atrocities: the brutalization of Indigenous children in residential schools, the child sex abuse scandals and cover-ups, the homophobia and misogyny. We were also fed up with its obsession with abortion. When we attended Catholic schools (first grade through college for him, high school and college for me), the focus was on social justice and community service, not bus rides to Washington, D.C., to protest *Roe v. Wade*.

My father must have been crushed that I stopped attending Mass, although he never asked me about it. But at brunch that day in Rockport, frustrations of some sort burst through. I've thought about that trip many times over the years because my dad seemed irritated and angry during much of it. He enjoyed being by the ocean and eating fresh seafood. He enjoyed going for long walks in the morning. He enjoyed reading and chatting on the porch of my aunt and uncle's cottage, where we were staying. And although he resisted the idea at first, he loved the sunset harbor cruise I insisted we take on the schooner *The Appledore*. But he got crabbier by the day and only cheered up when vacation was over and we arrived at Logan Airport for our flights home. Maybe he grew restless because the trip pulled him away from his research, or because it was quite expensive, or because I wasn't as friendly and companionable as I should have been. Maybe he and my mother weren't getting along—there had been some sort of kerfuffle about a train ride into Boston to visit old friends of hers. Whatever the reason or reasons, it makes me sad to think about.

So I think about O'Connor's stories and what my dad valued in them. He obviously knew of her devout Catholicism—thus his reserving a seat for her next to Merton in his pantheon of influential figures. And the parade of grotesque characters populating her stories, the troubling and bizarre goings-on? His sense of humor sometimes tilted toward the macabre, so I can see her winning him over in that respect as well. I like how my reading compels me to think about him in new ways and carry on our conversations about writers and books and stories, if only in my musings—and sometimes in my dreams.

Chapter 11

The New Basics Cookbook
by Julee Rosso & Sheila Lukins

Dear Kristin,
Good cookin'!
Merry Christmas, 1993

My mother hated cooking. She felt relieved when we kids were grown and out of the house so that she would no longer have to worry about dinner for five each night. She did have her strengths. She made a delicious Thanksgiving turkey. She enjoyed shopping for fresh produce at the farmers market. For a while, she had a garden and grew tomatoes and green beans—possibly other things, but that's what I remember. We always had fresh fruit in the house, even in winter thanks to mail-order delivery of oranges, tangerines, and grapefruits. I remember the excitement of opening the front door on snowy afternoons and finding the wooden crate full of Florida bounty on the porch. And she loved setting a festive holiday table with fine china, sterling silverware, crystal wine glasses, and beautiful tablecloths. She was a bit less interested in the food.

She did her best to shake things up and cut down on prepping, buying packaged kits for tacos and gyros and a crockpot that could do the cooking for her while she was at work. Every now and then, she'd make her version of slumgullion: ground beef, canned corn, and a few other ingredients mixed together in a skillet. She also baked our birthday cakes when we were little. I always thought they were homemade, but my sister remembers seeing boxed cake mixes. I'm certain the Christmas cookies we made each year were from scratch. If my brother or sister know otherwise, I would rather they not tell me. I can picture clear as day the cover of the Betty Crocker cookbook that was in the house. How often my mother used it, I don't know. Cooking was simply not her forte.

My sister says she believed vegetables came in cans until she went off to college. Lettuce meant iceberg, and she only knew about the existence of spinach from *Popeye* cartoons. She remembers a transformative experience when she was a teenager and watched our Aunt Cecily sauté onions, peppers, and sausages together. The aromas! The flavors! She said she never knew such a thing was possible. I don't think our mother was *that* bad in the kitchen, but I did used to say that my lack of cooking skills must be inherited from my mother. In fact, my mother used to say that about *her* mother. I can't use that excuse, though, because my sister is a fantastic cook, self-taught by watching *The French Chef* and reading *Gourmet* and *Bon Appetit*. She and her husband have an entire bookcase dedicated to cookbooks.

I know that time, effort, precision, and care go into cooking well, but my sister always makes it look easy. I remember a time when everyone gathered at my parents' house for a week in the summer. She, her husband, and two young sons had flown in from Seattle, and their flights and connections had turned into a disaster, with delay after delay. Yet right after they finally arrived in South Bend, she and I went to the grocery store to get ingredients for a spinach lasagna. When we got back home, she stood in the kitchen following a recipe on her phone. She made a great meal for a big group of people after traveling across the country and barely sleeping for 24 hours. I made the salad, my usual contribution. That and cleaning up afterwards.

*****

My mother gave me *The New Basics Cookbook* for Christmas in 1993, when I was 24 years old. Paul and I had moved into an apartment together that summer and were getting the hang of preparing meals at home. Our Catholic parents weren't thrilled that we decided to live together before we were married, but after speaking their piece, just once when we first told them our plans, they let it go and were nothing but loving and supportive. Giving me the cookbook may have been my mother's way of encouraging us in our new life together. Looking at the book now, I'm beset with a bundle of emotions. Happiness as I recall my family's joyful Christmases. Guilt for not using the cookbook more. Failure for following in my mother's footsteps in the culinary realm. Fear that if I attempt a recipe, I'll screw it up. Curiosity: What's the worst that could happen? What if I surprised Paul or a small group of friends with a wonderful home-cooked meal? They would be thrilled—and would probably pass out from shock.

Paul especially made good use of the cookbook in those early years. He had learned to cook from his mother and enjoyed shopping for fresh ingredients and trying new recipes—still does. I was always by his side during meal prep—still am. I'm the sous chef, rinsing vegetables, chopping, dicing. And I ask questions: How long did you cook it on each side? How often are you stirring that? What temperature does that bake at? But then I can never remember. It's not that I'm (wholly) uninterested in cooking. It's that I feel utterly inept, like when I walk into a garden center in the spring, scan the beautiful plants, flowers, and trees, and think, "Well, what can I bring home and kill?" I also lack a key quality when it comes to cooking: patience. Years ago, my friend Sinane put her hand on my knee and said, "Honey, patience is not one of your virtues." We burst out laughing. She was right.

*****

I open *The New Basics* today and head to the index to look for our favorite recipes. There aren't many. Of course, the book is full of wonderful recipes, but we only tried a handful. A lot of them call for umpteen ingredients we either couldn't find or couldn't afford. But I turn to the tried and true, the rumpled, stained pages attesting to our efforts. Page 136, Broccoli and Garlic Penne. Page 328, Red Beans and Rice. Page 518, Vegetable Chili. These were a few of our go-tos. One night when Paul was out, I made an apple pie from scratch, including dough mixed with bits of cheddar cheese: Page 716, Apple of Her Eye Pie. It was the first and last pie I ever made. It wasn't pretty, but it tasted like apple pie, which I considered a victory. In fact, I enjoy baking. I make a great pumpkin bread around the holidays (with a recipe from another cookbook my mother gave me, published by the Junior League of South Bend). I used to bake Tollhouse cookies and oatmeal raisin cookies every now and then. I recently tried a blueberry muffin recipe. Long ago, I made gingersnaps for an office holiday cookie exchange. Like the pie, they weren't pretty—gingerblobs, really—but they tasted fine. I haven't baked much since being diagnosed with dozens of food allergies, including milk/butter.

I actually can't cite too many kitchen disasters. I haven't burned anything. Pots and pans don't overflow. Soufflés don't collapse. Pot roast isn't overdone—because I've not attempted any of it. There have been unfortunate incidents, however. I forgot to add the flour once when baking cookies. I neglected to remove the cardboard base when sticking a frozen pizza in the oven. I made a pot of coffee at my in-laws' house one morning, but I used a serving spoon rather than a tablespoon to dole out the grounds, so the pot overflowed and made a mess. I tried to flip a pancake, maybe that same weekend, but was so afraid of messing it up in front of everyone, I handed the spatula off to someone else. What kind of adult is afraid to flip a pancake? When my friends talk about cooking—trying out a new soup, stew, or pastry recipe, or making Thai, Indian, or Brazilian food, I love hearing about it but remain silent. I'm not sure they grasp the depths of my inexperience.

I have to say I can feed myself just fine. I can scramble, fry, and boil eggs; bake or sauté fish; steam and roast vegetables; bake a potato; sauté garlic to mix with pretty much anything; make pesto (in a blender); and get creative with salads. When I went home years ago to help care for my mother after her spinal surgery, I did all the cooking for my parents. I made a quiche. I cooked steak and fish. I steamed vegetables and made rice. I kept us all fed for two weeks, and no one was poisoned or malnourished. But it was a relief when Paul picked me up to head back to our house and I didn't have to do it anymore. That's what my mother always said: that she resented it because it was something she *had* to do after a long day's work. Of course, it wasn't every night. On Fridays, we brought in a pizza or went to Barnaby's for burgers and fries, and as my brother, sister, and I got older, our family went out to eat more often. My father grilled burgers in the summer and made chili in the winter. His specialty when my mom was out of town or indisposed was buttered egg noodles—kid food that we loved. One winter, he went on a bread-baking spree. In time, my sister probably helped with dinner. Every so often, I "made" the pasta.

In the 1970s, I'm pretty sure the only pasta on midwestern America's radar was spaghetti, always with marina from a jar. I boiled the water, overcooked the noodles, and heated the sauce. I remember my mom telling me to rinse the noodles in the colander after straining them. Was that a thing? I can still see the look on my brother's face as he tried to choke down the limp, cold spaghetti strands. I guess what I'm saying is, I tried to help. Nowadays, I still blunder. If I head to the grocery store, I end up texting Paul because I can't find this or that, or I don't know what to substitute if something's not in stock, or I come home having forgotten to buy an item on the list, or I buy the wrong thing. I can never remember which type of ground turkey I'm supposed to get.

My mother had some pretty good cooking/kitchen fails—like microwaving salmon. At least, placing a beautiful cut of salmon in the microwave strikes me as a horrifying thing to do. She once picked up a cake with buttercream frosting from the bakery, stuck it in the trunk of her car, and proceeded to run errands for a couple of hours in 90-degree heat. The cake looked great, but by that point, we were afraid to eat it. When Paul and I were engaged, my friend Cece and her mother threw a wedding shower for me in South Bend. My sister-in-law, her mother, my friend Traci, and I drove in from Chicago. Paul's mother took the train in from Detroit and stayed at my parents' house, as did Traci and I. The shower was in the afternoon, and that night, my mom made dinner for Paul's mom, Traci, and me, serving salmon and broccoli. There may also have been slices of bread at the table. The meal was fine but not quite enough. About an hour later, Traci pulled me aside and said, "I'm STARVING," so we got in the car and drove to Burger King. She kept apologizing, said she didn't mean to be rude, but I assured her it was okay—that this sort of thing had happened before.

To this day, Paul's haunted by the Thanksgiving we spent with my parents when after dinner, my mother shoved all the leftovers except the turkey down the garbage disposal. Broccoli, mashed potatoes, stuffing, corn, cranberry sauce—food for several meals all literally down the drain. "No one's going to eat it," she said. "Just get rid of it." And he will never forget the time we were at my parents' house for the weekend, and he pre-heated the oven to warm up leftover pizza for lunch. When he heard the beep, he opened the oven door to find an array of dishes on the rack, now burning hot. "Um," he said. "Oh, are those still in there?" my mom asked. "I stashed them there last week to clear the kitchen counters for the cleaning woman." As my brother-in-law once said, "You should have spent a bit more time in home-ec, Nan." She was always good-natured about the teasing—and she wasn't alone in her aversion to cooking. She would tell of a time when she was with her friend Connie while another friend talked about making spaghetti sauce. She and Connie looked at each other. "*Make* spaghetti sauce?" they asked. Traci once told me that when she mentioned to her mother how hard it was to make a pie crust, her mother responded, "What are you, crazy? Just buy the pre-made ones!"

*****

I wonder if my mother's stance toward cooking stemmed in part from her 1970s feminist activism—a conviction that women had to get out of the kitchen if they were to be taken seriously and achieve equal footing with men in the work force. Hillary Rodham Clinton expressed the same sentiment in 1992 when her husband was running for president. "I suppose I could have stayed home and baked cookies and had teas," she infamously responded to a query about her career, "but what I decided to do was to fulfill my profession." As Amy Chozick writes in her November 5, 2016, *New York Times* piece, "Hillary Clinton and the Return of the (Unbaked) Cookies," "The blowback was intense and she spent weeks apologizing, saying that she respected women who chose to stay at home and raise children. *Family Circle* magazine invited her and Barbara Bush to submit recipes for a chocolate-chip cookie bake-off, and she obliged." That the *New York Times* saw fit to run such a piece three days before Clinton faced Trump in the presidential election speaks volumes about the anxiety, misogyny, and clickbait potential surrounding what remains a hot-button issue.

An internet search on "cooking and feminism" yields a slew of results: a recent doctoral dissertation, *Recipes for Resistance: Feminist Political Discourse About Cooking: 1870-1985*, along with dozens of articles and essays from blogs, newsletters, magazines, and academic journals. Titles include "Reclaim the Kitchen: How Cooking and Feminism Can Coexist," "A Feminist Guide to Cooking," "Is Cooking Anti-Feminist?," "A New Discourse on the Kitchen: Feminism and Environmental Education," "'I'm not a feminist . . . I love cooking!' Why Food is a Feminist Issue," and "Has Feminism Killed the Art of Home Cooking?" In "Cook Thy Meal, Love Thy Body: Why I am a Feminist Who Cooks," Akanksha Mishra declares, "cooking has gone hand in hand with my feminist awakening." Sometimes, women follow more circuitous routes into the kitchen.

In "I Thought Cooking Would Make Me a Bad Feminist," published in *Bon Appetit* in 2017, Julia Black discusses her grandmother, who was a wonderful cook, and her mother, who was not. "While I think my grandmother always saw cooking as her intrinsic duty, I think my mother saw cooking as a trap designed to keep her from more intellectual pursuits," she writes. Black's musings strike a chord as I suspect my mother might have felt the same. She had a family and a full-time job, and she read voraciously, requiring long stretches of peace and quiet. She wasn't interested in spending time in the kitchen. She would not accept it as her destiny.

Neither will Julia Black, up to a point. "As for me," she continues, "I can easily dismiss the old-fashioned idea that, based on a pair of matching chromosomes, I have the responsibility to know how to make a soufflé. But, at the same time, I've often felt ashamed for lacking the kind of basic domestic knowledge many women are taught by more housework-oriented moms than mine." For a while, being "too busy to cook" was a point of pride for Black, but eventually, she came to believe otherwise. "Cooking, like feminism, can take many forms," she decides. "It can be an act of nurturing, a statement of love, a playground for experimentation, or a method of self-care. No woman should be shamed into cooking, and no women should be shamed out of it."

Aurvi Sharma wasn't so much shamed into cooking as compelled toward it as a practical matter. In her 2021 *Bon Appetit* article, "I

Rejected Cooking in the Name of Feminism—Until I Had To," she recounts her peripatetic childhood in India due to her father's job as "an engineer with the government. . . . Moving across 11 cities and seven schools, my mother's food was the constant that steadied me." As a teenager, though, she came to view cooking as anathema to feminism, a stance she clung to until moving to England at age 22 for a graduate writing program. There, she realized she couldn't feed herself properly. "For the first month I subsisted on soggy heat-and-eat pastas that I hid under a shower of chile flakes," she writes. Reaching rock-bottom, she "unpacked the spices my mother had placed in my luggage" and ventured into her dorm's kitchen, burning and scorching her way through early attempts to recreate the meals of her childhood. She finally called her mother to ask for help. "Over the next few weeks, my mother taught me how to cook by sight, smell, touch, and instinct," she says. "As we cooked together we reminisced."

Listening to her mother's stories, Sharma reaches a deeper understanding of her female cultural heritage, and a greater appreciation for the "village grandmothers" who found "power" and "respite" in the kitchen. "The women sang, swapped life stories, and corralled relief in their culinary sisterhood," she explains, "a smidgeon of agency in a culture that repeatedly denied them. . . . When I was ready for it, my mother passed this legacy to me." I possess no such legacy from my mother, and like my mother, I have been teased for being a bad cook, or no cook at all. I'm appalled yet not surprised that the stigma persists well into the twenty-first century. Like handling Saran Wrap, facing such criticism can be maddening. Women have responded in myriad ways over the years.

The suffragettes encountered extreme vitriol in their fight for equality as critics fomented fear and hatred of "unsexed" women abdicating their wifely responsibilities. Cartoons, posters, and postcards of the time presented caricatures of women stomping off to the voting booth, leaving spouses and children behind to wallow in backed-up household chores. A 1906 postcard called "When Women Vote" depicts composed, elegantly dressed young women smoking and playing cards while a harried man in the background holds a squalling baby and rinses diapers in a bucket. Another postcard, "Mother's Got the Habit Now," from 1913 shows a woman in men's clothing smoking and briskly striding out of the house, a "Votes for Women" sash draped around her chest. An emasculated man in pink, much smaller in stature, sits cowering and rocking a baby in a cradle.

Some women strived to assure the public they had not lost sight of their womanly duties—but with a twist. "How Suffragists Used Cookbooks as a Recipe for Subversion," by Nina Martyris, explores the "half-dozen cookbooks published by suffragette associations" between 1886 and 1920, when the 19th Amendment was passed. The cookbooks raised money for charitable causes, as culinary archivist Jan Longone explains, but also served as "a strategic rebuttal to the snide jokes and hurtful innuendo directed against suffragists, who were painted as neglectful mothers and kitchen-hating harridans." *The Woman's Suffrage Cook Book* of 1886 contained recipes contributed by "regular housewives," "prominent suffragettes," and career women such as "Chicago obstetrician and gynecologist Alice Bunker Stockham, the fifth woman to become a licensed doctor in the U.S.," who contributed a recipe for Coraline Cake. "Dr. Stockham was anti-alcohol and anti-corset but—extraordinarily for her time—pro-masturbation. She publicly endorsed it as healthy for both men and women." Cora Scott Pond, a "real estate investor who had refused to wear a corset starting at the age of 16," provided a recipe for Irish stew. By virtue of association, *The Woman's Suffrage Cook Book* was a radical publication.

Along with recipes, *The Holiday Gift Cook Book* of 1891 included "pro-suffrage quotes by famous people," and *The Suffrage Cook Book* of 1915 offered "recipes, celebrity endorsements, photographs and saucy jokes" as well as "recipes carrying playful titles like 'Hymen Cake,' 'Mother's Election Cake,' 'Suffrage Salad Dressing,' 'Suffrage Angel Cake' and 'Parliament Gingerbread (With apologies to the English Suffragists).'" The book included satirical recipes, too. Ingredients for "Pie for a Suffragist's Doubting Husband" include "War, White Slavery, Child Labor, . . . Poisonous Water, [and] Impure Food" with instructions to "Mix the crust with tact and velvet gloves, using no sarcasm, especially with the upper crust. Upper crusts must be handled with extreme care, for they quickly sour if manipulated roughly."

I love the fighting spirit, sense of humor, and dedication to the cause infusing these books.

Yet such efforts did little to dispel stereotypes of women who defied the norms—that they were unnatural, monsters, not real women. Born in 1932, Sylvia Plath suffered great psychological harm from society's harassment and oppression of ambitious women, particularly if they were brilliant prize-winning writers. She adopted a tactic similar to some of her suffragist foremothers and Victorian-era women as well. As Deborah Lutz explains, "writer and leading intellectual" Harriet Martineau "prided herself in not embodying the dreaded stereotype of the time: 'a literary lady who could not sew.' Glad to be a contradiction, she could not only write but also 'make shirts and puddings, and iron and mend, and get my bread by my needle, if necessary.'" Plath, too, determined to assert her traditional womanly bona fides. "Don't worry that I am a 'career woman,'" she wrote to her mother from Cambridge University in 1956. "I am definitely meant to be married & have children & a home & write like these women I admire," she states, naming several female authors. "She had a horror of ending up alone, a 'career girl,'" Heather Clark explains in *Red Comet: The Short Life and Blazing Art of Sylvia Plath.* "In her journal she wrote, 'Save me from that, that final wry sour lemon acid in the veins of single clever lonely women.' Sylvia, along with her contemporaries, had been socially conditioned to think this way. . . . The women students [at Cambridge] may have discussed their intellectual ambitions over tea, but they were not encouraged to question the established hierarchies."

Plath did question the hierarchies, of course, fiercely, throughout her life and writing, yet her journals contain derisive remarks about unmarried women and childless women. For her part, she married, had two babies in quick succession, and became hell-bent on doing it all: raising children, cooking, cleaning, sewing, gardening, and renovating and decorating the stately but tumble-down, freezing-in-winter Devon cottage she and Ted Hughes moved into in the summer of '61. For the time period, Hughes was an extraordinarily involved father, and Plath sometimes had household help, yet trying to perform countless chores to perfection while raising two children proved arduous. On top of it all, she needed the time, privacy, and mental energy to write, establishing a routine whereby she wrote in the mornings while Ted tended the children and vice versa in the afternoons. "Plath's study was her sanctuary," Clark states. "Her mornings there were 'as peaceful as churchgoing—the red plush rug and all, and the feeling that nothing else but writing and thinking is done there, no sleeping, eating or mundane stuff.'" She wrote and published several of her best poems that spring, including "Tulips" and "The Colossus." Yet the balancing act remained a constant struggle.

I thought of my mother while reading *Red Comet* as she and Plath were contemporaries, born just a year apart. They also had much in common: a Massachusetts upbringing, a summer job at the seaside (live-in nannying for Plath, waitressing for my mother), majoring in English at a women's college (Plath attended Smith in Northampton; my mom went to Emmanuel in Boston, which is now co-ed), and coming of age amid narrow expectations for women. There's a photograph somewhere of my mother as a smiling, bikini-clad, deeply tanned teenager at the beach that mirrors such photos of Plath. There are so many questions I want to ask my mom about her young womanhood especially. But I can't. There's not much left to say about that.

*****

There is a bit more to say about my kitchen/cooking anxieties. Paul and I used to love watching Anthony Bourdain's shows. I remember him saying in one episode, "Everyone should know how to make a nice meal for a group of friends." I felt as if he'd broken the fourth wall, looked right at me, pointed, and said, "J'accuse!" because I don't know if I could do much more for my friends than boil a pot of water for pasta and make a salad. Does that count as a nice meal? Close friends from high school and I have begun getting together for a weekend every summer. Two of them are amazing cooks who bring coolers and containers with enough food to feed an army. They chop, marinate, simmer, grill, and baste. They incorporate wonderful spices. They bake complicated things generally only seen in upscale pastry shops. Like my sister, they make it look elegant and easy. I, on the other hand, bring tortilla chips, salsa, eggs, and fruit to our reunions.

My friend Mia and I commiserate as she claims to know nothing about cooking, either. "I tried cooking an egg and the yolk broke," she said of one attempt. "Then I tried cooking bacon, and I burned it." Her mother came out to see what was going on. "What are you *doing*?" she asked. "I'm just trying to feed myself!" Mia wailed.

*****

After my mom died, I wrote a few poems about her, including this one offering a different way of thinking about what it means to nourish a family. All our lives, she fed us well.

Sustenance

My mother hated cooking
this was well known
joked about over the years

a punchline

I guess it's pretty funny
a woman who doesn't like to cook
yet I recall a feast on

our dining room table

books and magazines
notepad, typewriter, letters
envelopes and stamps

women standing, planning
cigarette smoke swirling around
their heads late into the night

my brother, sister, and I asleep
in our beds as they strived
for fair play, for equality

It's where she sat
one night each month
to pay bills

Christmas Eve, we were banished
from the room as she wrapped presents
paper, tags, ribbons strewn around her

I keep my dining room table clear
hers feeds me still

Chapter 12

Rubáiyát of Omar Khayyám
Rendered into English verse by Edmund Fitzgerald

Dear Kristin,
I think 17 is the
perfect age to read this.
I hope you love it.
Love on Christmas,
Mother
1986

I love my mother's sweet inscription in this book, but I'm surprised she thought 17 would be the right age for me to read *Rubáiyát of Omar Khayyám*. I can't imagine I would have recognized, let alone appreciated, the verses' "fusion of sadness and delight" as it says on the back of my beautiful edition with illustrations by Edmund Dulac, a French-British artist whose first commission was for illustrated editions of the Brontë novels—how fitting that things are circling back to the Brontës, where it all began. The dust jacket and cloth covers are a saturated burgundy with elegant gold lettering designed by Tony Selina of the Old Goat Graphic Company. I had to look up such a fantastic name and came upon Selina's obituary in *The Guardian*, written by his brother, Howard.

Tony was a bit of a Renaissance man, with wide-ranging interests and talents. "After a spell as the head of design at Kogan Page," Howard writes, ". . . Tony set up the Old Goat Graphic Company [in London, England], a one-man operation with a small but chaotic studio space at Clerkenwell Workshops. It was from here that he produced many of the covers used by Wordsworth Press in their Children's Classics series, as well as jackets for a host of other titles." The obituary ends on a forlorn note. "Tony was a larger-than-life character who will be quietly missed by a great many people, although, of his family, I am the only one to survive him."

Rubáiyát of Omar Khayyám is another one I didn't read for decades. I always enjoyed looking at it and feeling its heft in my hands, and it had pride of place on bookshelves in my homes over the years. But I only read it for the first time a couple of years ago, turning to it in the evenings after a long day's work when my brain felt tired—after nearly two years of the pandemic, and after becoming increasingly disenchanted with my job. I was in the mood for soothing verses, and as I began reading the quatrains, I became enthralled. I'm not sure whether they capture, reflect, or spur my own "fusion of sadness and delight." Perhaps all three.

I knew nothing about Omar Khayyám or Edward Fitzgerald when I received the book. I still didn't when I picked it up recently to read it again for this project. Turning to the internet, I learn that Omar Khayyám was an 11th- and 12th-century (1048-1131) Persian astronomer, astrologer, philosopher, physician, mathematician, and poet in the Sufi tradition. Edmund Fitzgerald (often written as FitzGerald) was a Victorian poet and writer best known for his translation of Khayyám's verses from Persian to English. "Loose translations" seems more like it. "To a large extent," I read on GradeSaver.com, which carries a disclaimer saying they got the information from Wikipedia, "the *Rubaiyat* can be considered original poetry by FitzGerald loosely based on Omar's quatrains rather than a 'translation' in the narrow sense. FitzGerald was open about the liberties he had taken with his source material." Many have also questioned whether FitzGerald could have fully understood the Sufism imbuing the verses. If not, his renderings of the quatrains become ever more dubious.

Controversy swirls not only around FitzGerald's translation practices but also around Khayyám and whether the verses are even his to begin with. As I learned on Wikipedia, scholars have noted the verses' "lack of linguistic homogeneity and continuity of ideas," suggesting authors other than or in addition to Khayyám.

Sadegh Hedayat, an early 20th-century Iranian writer and translator, believed just "14 quatrains could be attributed to Khayyám with certainty" among the more than 1200 that have at times been ascribed to him. Others say 36, or 121, or 178 quatrains may be his. The man himself proves equally elusive. "Different biographers have documented him as a fun-loving, wine-drinking agnostic; a closet Zoroastrian; a Sufi Muslim; an orthodox Sunni Moslem; and a follower of Ancient Greek philosophy. All agree that he was an outstanding intellectual," says FamousScientists.org.

Where does all this take me? Down a long and winding rabbit hole if I let it, but I've been wondering if I should put the brakes on that sort of thing. Lately, when I look around at all my books, I feel a tinge of despair along with excitement and curiosity. We have so much wonderful reading material at arm's reach, not to mention the seven boxes of books stashed in our hall closet because our apartment can only hold so many bookcases, I can't imagine ever getting through it all. The thought of ancillary material makes me anxious and calls to mind Henry Bemis from the "Time Enough at Last" episode of *The Twilight Zone*—a 24-minute horror show for anyone who lives to read.

Portrayed by Burgess Meredith with aching sincerity, all Henry wants to do is read and share his joy of reading with others, but he's continually thwarted by his wife, his boss, his customers at the bank—Philistines all who don't see the point of modern poetry or Dickens' colorful characters and who fire off the greatest insult they can think of: "You, Mr. Bemis, are a *reader*!" When a nuclear explosion leaves Henry alone in a wasted landscape, he contemplates suicide as the loneliness settles in. Just as he's about to pull the trigger of a pistol he found, he sees that the public library remains partially intact, with hundreds of tomes littering the ground. He begins sorting the books and maps out a schedule. There's a pile for February, March, April, and so on. But he stumbles, and his thick glasses fall off and shatter, leaving him unable to read. "That's not fair," he says in tears. "That's not fair at all." Indeed.

So here I am reading obituaries and thinking of the most—to me—terrifying and heartbreaking episode of *The Twilight Zone*. Time now to turn to the *Rubáiyát*, which luxuriates in the *carpe diem* tradition: Seize the day, for tomorrow we die, its 110 quatrains emphatically stress. Each one notes the fleetingness of our days that all the soul-searching and philosophizing in the world won't change, regardless of what organized religion would have us believe. The first quatrain heralds the rising sun, while in the last, the speaker bids his beloved to visit his grave with joy in their heart and a glass of wine in their hand to be drunk and turned over, empty.

Quatrain I establishes the tone: "Wake! For the Sun behind on Eastern height / Has chased the Session of the Stars from Night; / And, to the field of Heav'n ascending, strikes / The Sultán's Turret with a Shaft of Light." We'll come to see that whether Sultan or serf, the same fate awaits us all. Quatrains II and III present another key motif: the tavern as site of fellowship, fun, and enlightenment:

Before the phantom of the False morning died,
Methought a Voice within the Tavern cried,
"When all the Temple is prepared within,
Why lags the drowsy Worshipper outside?"
And, as the Cock crew, those who stood before
The Tavern shouted—"Open then the door!
You know how little while we have to stay,
And, once departed, may return no more."

Thus unfolds a series of reminders and guidance on how to make the most of our brief time on earth. Don't waste a single moment. Appreciate the small, simple joys of the everyday. And drink the wine. Always, drink the wine.

I have a hard time choosing which verses to quote, they're all so moving and meaningful. Quatrain XII offers an ode to life's simple pleasures: "Here with a little Bread beneath the Bough, / A Flask of Wine, a Book of Verse—and Thou / Beside me singing in the Wilderness— / Oh, Wilderness were Paradise enow!" Quatrain XIV is among many discouraging us from dwelling on the future, for in doing so, we waste precious time and lose out on all the present moment has to offer: "Were it not Folly, Spider-like to spin / The Thread of present Life away to win— / What? for ourselves, who know not if we shall / Breathe out the very Breath we now breathe in!" Quatrain XXI strikes a similar note, while XXIV is among those acknowledging the endgame for us all: the grave, presented nevertheless as a site of beauty and growth: "I sometimes think that never blows so red / The Rose as where some buried Caesar bled; / that every Hyacinth the Garden wears / Dropt in her Lap from some once lovely Head." Why and how does the grave produce beauty? Because of the mourners who hold the dead in their memories? Because the dead make way for the living? I'm not entirely sure, and I appreciate the musings engendered by such ideas. Quatrain XXVI presents a more somber concept of death: "Ah, make the most of what we yet may spend, / Before we too into the Dust descend; / Dust into Dust, and under Dust, to life, / Sans Wine, sans Song, sans Singer, and—sans End!"

Quatrains XXIX and XXX are among those enjoining us to stop seeking answers to our existential questions for the simple fact that there aren't any. The learned and holy possess no more knowledge about the meaning of life, or what happens when we die, than anyone else. We waste our time turning to them when we ought to stay focused on the here and now:

Why, all the Saints and Sages who discuss'd
Of the Two Worlds so learnedly, are thrust
Like foolish Prophets forth; their Words to Scorn
Are scatter'd, and their Mouths are stopt with Dust.
Myself when young did eagerly frequent
Doctor and Saint, and hear great argument
About it and about: but evermore
Came out by the same door as in I went.

I like the "About it and about," reflecting the circuitous, fruitless yammering of the "wise."

I'm reminded of a key passage in Virginia Woolf's *To the Lighthouse*. Part II of the novel, "Time Passes," focuses on the Ramsay family's seaside summer home during a ten-year stretch when it was largely devoid of human beings. A description of the wind howling around the house at night leads to thoughts on the human compulsion for truth-seeking:

Also the sea tosses itself and breaks itself, and should any sleeper fancying that he might find on the beach an answer to his doubts, a sharer of his solitude, throw off his bedclothes and go down by himself to walk on the sand, no image with semblance of serving and divine promptitude comes readily to hand bringing the night to order and making the world reflect the compass of the soul. The hand dwindles in his hand; the voice bellows in his ear. Almost it would appear that it is useless in such confusion to ask the night those questions as to what, and why, and wherefore, which tempt the sleeper from his bed to seek an answer.

According to Quatrains XXXII and XXXIII of the *Rubáiyát*, it is not only useless but also insolent to ask such questions. "Into this Universe," XXXII begins, picking up where XXXI leaves off, "and *Why* not knowing, / Nor *Whence*, like Water willy-nilly flowing: / And out of it, as Wind along the Waste, / I know not *Whither*, willy-nilly blowing." XXXIII goes on: "What, without asking, hither hurried *Whence*? / And, without asking, *Whither* hurried hence! / Ah, contrite Heav'n endowed us with the Vine / To drug the memory of that insolence!" Yet both the *Rubáiyát* and *To the Lighthouse* cite blazing moments of awareness and truth. We just have to know where to look for them.

Quatrain LXXXIII declares that catching "the one True Light" in the tavern, even just a fleeting glimpse of it, regardless of its effect on us, is better than seeking and never finding it in the temple: "And this I know: whether the one True Light, / Kindle to Love, or Wrath-consume me quite, / One Flash of It within the Tavern caught / Better than in the Temple lost outright." In fact, Quatrain LXXXVI declares, there is more justice and forgiveness in the tavern than the temple. In the third and final section of *To the Lighthouse*, Lily Briscoe stands painting on the Ramsays' lawn, looking back and forth between her canvas and the drawing-room steps of their home. Her thoughts evoke and carry on the quotation from "Time Passes":

And, resting . . . the old question which traversed the sky of the soul perpetually . . . stood over her, paused over her, darkened over her. What is the meaning of life? That was all—a simple question; one that tended to close in on one with years. The great revelation had never come. The great revelation perhaps never did come. Instead there were little daily miracles, illuminations, matches struck unexpectedly in the dark . . . this was of the nature of a revelation. In the midst of chaos there was shape . . .

I cling to these words from the *Rubáiyát* and from Woolf, which make it possible to contend with the loss of my parents along with an increasingly catastrophic world. Every day, I do my best to recognize and embrace the "little daily miracles," which isn't hard to do because there are so many. Laughing with my husband. Getting a text from a friend. Walking by the sea. Looking up from a book to savor a phrase or a scene. Petting my cats. When I find myself growing morose and missing my parents, I sometimes let myself ride out the emotions, for there's no shame in missing them. There better not be, because I will think about them and miss them every day for the rest of my life. But I try to reorient myself to the present with a dual-meaning mantra, "Right this moment," intoned when I'm out for a walk or trying to fall asleep at night. Fretting about something I said weeks, months, or years ago? Worrying about what may happen weeks, months, or years from now? It saps me of energy and wastes precious moments that the *Rubáiyát* reminds me I can never get back.

These verses have come to me, or I to them, at just the right time, I think. Reading them at 17 or in my twenties would have been lovely, I'm sure. But now, after losses and heartache, they mean more than they would have then, and they become interwoven with other books and poems I've read, like Mary Oliver's "The Summer Day," whose speaker describes a grasshopper in sharp detail and then reflects on how we choose to spend our days:

I do know how to pay attention, how to fall down
into the grass, how to kneel down in the grass,
how to be idle and blessed, how to stroll through the fields,
which is what I have been doing all day.
Tell me, what else should I have done?

Doesn't everything die at last, and too soon?
Tell me, what is it you plan to do
with your one wild and precious life?

Quatrain LVI expresses a similar sentiment: "Waste not your Hour, nor in the vain pursuit / Of This and That endeavour and dispute; / Better be merry with the fruitful Grape / Than sadden after none, or bitter, Fruit."

Poets throughout history and all over the world have explored the various themes at play in the *Rubáiyát*. To my eyes and ears, the quatrains rehearse English poetry in particular, lending further insight, perhaps, into the controversies surrounding FitzGerald's "translations." For starters, the quatrains are in iambic pentameter, first used by Geoffrey Chaucer in the 14th century. They're Shakespearean, evoking the sonnets' juxtaposition of human mortality with the power and longevity of poetry. Their *carpe diem* spirit evokes Christopher Marlowe's "The Passionate Shepherd to His Love" and especially Andrew Marvell's "To His Coy Mistress," in which the speaker urges his love to be/sleep with him *now*, for time's a-wasting. "Now let us sport us while we may, / And now, like amorous birds of prey, / Rather at once our time devour / Than languish in his slow-chapped power." Like many quatrains in the *Rubáiyát*, Alexander Pope's *Essay on Man* chastises us humans for our hubris, for never being satisfied with what we have and for lamenting that we cannot see into the future. If we could, the poem explains, we would lose all hope and be fearful and miserable each day.

The opening of Quatrain CVIII evokes Matthew Arnold's "Dover Beach," a poem I have loved for years and that guts me even more now that I live by the sea. "Ah Love!" the quatrain begins, "could you and I with Fate conspire / To grasp this sorry Scheme of Things entire, / Would not we shatter it to bits—and then / Re-mould it nearer to the Heart's Desire!" As Pope admonishes, however, we should never desire to know the future, and as Arnold proclaims—as does Woolf in *To the Lighthouse*—we stand defenseless against the ravages of nature. "Ah, love," Arnold writes in the last stanza of "Dover Beach," "let us be true / To one another! for the world, which seems / To lie before us like a land of dreams, / So various, so beautiful, so new, / Hath really neither joy, nor love, nor light, / Nor certitude, nor peace, nor help for pain; / And we are here as on a darkling plain." In my survey of English literature class, "Dover Beach" came around in Unit Three on the Victorian Age, late in the semester when so many of us were hanging on by a thread. The poem never fails to strike a powerful chord with students, always generating impassioned discussion and writing.

The speaker of "Dover Beach" expresses this grim outlook on life after hearing the noise of the sea. "Listen! you hear the grating roar / Of pebbles which the waves draw back, and fling / At their return, up the high strand, / Begin, and cease, and then again begin, / With tremulous cadence slow, and bring / The eternal note of sadness in." Just when I'm trying to lighten up a little, this poem's sad undertow pulls me back, and I reflect on walking with my brother along Cape Hedge beach in Rockport, Massachusetts. It was an overcast, blustery afternoon, with crashing waves bigger than any I'd seen since moving to the area a couple of months earlier. The thunderous, crackling sound of the water pulling along the rocks at the shore was beautiful, haunting, and yes, a little melancholy as my brother and I found ourselves torn between the joy of being together in Rockport, site of our magical childhood summer vacations, and grief over the loss of our parents. In that moment, we especially missed our mother, who loved Rockport so much. Together, we felt the "fusion of sadness and delight," as did my sister and I when she and her husband visited in August. We all went out to dinner on August 2nd, our mother's birthday. We toasted her and thought of her the next day as we strolled around Rockport enjoying the breathtaking vistas.

The *Rubáiyát* offers so much more to ponder. That there's a "Master of a Show," and we're all just pawns in his game. That we have no control whatsoever over our lives despite our best efforts to convince ourselves otherwise. That today's blooming rose is neither the wilted one of yesterday nor the budding one of tomorrow but its own entity moving through the cycle of life. And that when it's our time to die—time to drink wine from the cup for the last time—we mustn't shrink from it or fear it, for it's a natural experience and part of what makes us fully human.

The penultimate verse, Quatrain CIX, states what no one with a spouse/partner/significant other, whomever it may be, ever wants to acknowledge: one of the two will die first. "But see! The rising Moon of Heav'n again / Looks for us, Sweet-heart, through the quivering Plane: / How oft hereafter rising will she look / Among those leaves—for one of us in vain!" The exclamation point highlights the significance of this fact, yet the final verse, Quatrain CX, exhorts happiness at the grave: "And when Yourself with silver Foot shall pass / Among the Guests Star-scatter'd on the Grass, / And in your joyous errand reach the spot / Where I made One—turn down an empty Glass!" Below the quatrain stands the book's final word, "TAMÁM," Arabic for "OK" or "all right."

Someday, I'll read more about Omar Khayyám, Edward FitzGerald, Sufism, and all manner of subjects that will shed further light on the provenance and meaning of *Rubáiyát of Omar Khayyám*. I can't help myself. It's what I do and who I am. I've read many times over the years that buying more books than you can possibly read is a sign of hope. It means "we're alive and curious," says the writer Laura Anne Bird, "and that we value other people's ideas. It means we aspire to nourish our brains with wisdom and poetry. It means we appreciate being able to hold an entire universe right in the palm of our hand." Entering the universe of *Rubáiyát of Omar Khayyám* elicits myriad emotions, along with the will to cherish each moment and think of my parents with joy and gratitude. I'm glad I chose it for this book's final chapter and will return to it, and its absorbing illustrations, many times in the years to come.

Afterword

It's been three years since I began reading the books inscribed and given to me by my parents—a three-year journey through novels, short stories, poetry, history, cultural criticism, and a cookbook, and through realism both gritty and magical. I have an inkling of how Luka Khalifa must have felt on Resham the flying carpet. And I wonder now where all this leaves me, and what I might leave with you. Virginia Woolf engages in similar musings at the start of *A Room of One's Own* as she ponders the task and expectations before her in presenting a lecture on women and fiction, whatever that may mean. "I should never be able to fulfill what is, I understand, the first duty of a lecturer," she says, "—to hand you after an hour's discourse a nugget of pure truth to wrap up between the pages of your notebooks and keep on the mantelpiece forever." Like Woolf, I doubt whether I have any such nuggets to share. At the very least, I can try to articulate my own truth. First, let me backtrack a bit.

A few years ago, I published an essay on the sympathy letters my parents received on the death of their first child, Kristin, who died when she was three years old during surgery to correct scoliosis. While writing the essay, a coda of sorts to my book on the first Kristin, I researched attitudes toward death, grieving practices, cemetery design, and sympathy letter etiquette in 19th- and 20th-century America. I also read *The Dark Interval: Letters on Loss, Grief, and Transformation*, by Rainer Marie Rilke, hoping to understand how my parents might have felt about the expressions of sympathy they received from family and friends. I reflect on Rilke's letters now in light of my own grief.

As I wrote in my sympathy letter essay, "Expressing the Inexpressible," Rilke urges us to embrace our sorrow as part of life's multiplicity. "I want to encourage you in your pain," he writes to a friend whose brother died by suicide, "so that you will completely experience it in all its fullness, because as the experience of a new intensity it is a great *life* experience and leads everything back again to life." To the sister of a German poet killed in World War I, he writes, "What is here and now is after all, what has been given and is expected of us, and we must attempt to transform everything that happens to us into a new familiarity and friendliness with it." To a friend on the death of her father, he urges, "Get to the bottom of this intensity and have faith in what is most horrible, instead of fighting it off—it reveals itself for those who can trust it in spite of its overwhelming and dire appearance, as a kind of initiation." I sometimes worry that my ongoing despondency over the deaths of my parents is unusual or unhealthy. With Rilke's words in mind, I can grieve without piling on more pain by wondering if I'm doing something wrong.

Rilke also writes about our enduring relationships with the dead. "Haven't you felt your father's influence and compassion a thousand times from the universe where all, truly all, Sidie, is beyond loss?" he writes to a friend. "Don't believe that something that belongs to our pure realities could drop away and simply cease." What first struck me as an appealing but abstract idea now resonates strongly. Reading the books from my parents has without a doubt allowed me to nurture my relationship with them and get to know them better, for amid all the questions I should have asked but never did lie a few answers as well, like Thomas Merton's influence on my father, or how my mother embodied a 1970s mainstream feminist Zeitgeist. I have a greater sense of what they valued and how they saw the world. And how they created a safe, warm bubble for us to grow up in, although they couldn't (no one can) spare us from harsh realities over the years. In the pages of the books they gave me, I've had glimpses into their immediate families and friendships. I've been able to envision them on their own, young, and before or without spouse or kids. And I believe there are additional revelations to come as I have more inscribed books waiting to be discovered or delved into again.

Then there are the books from my parents that don't have inscriptions: a Hogarth Press uniform edition of *A Room of One's Own* that my mother got for me in London; a 1954/eighth-impression edition of Woolf's *Jacob's Room*, also from London; wonderful old editions of Edith Wharton's New York novels (still to be read); *A Literature of Their Own*, by Elaine Showalter; *Moonlight in Duneland: The Illustrated History of the Chicago South Shore and South Bend Railroad*, by Ronald D. Cohen and Stephen G. McShane; William Trevor's last book of stories; an illustrated edition of *Daisy Miller*; *How to Massage Your Cat*, by Alice M. Brock; Grove Press's four-volume centenary edition of Samuel Beckett's complete works; and *Paw Prints in the Moonlight: The Heartwarming True Story of One Man and His Cat*, by Denis O'Connor, given to me by my dad one Christmas. He must have picked it up on his annual Christmas Eve dash to the Notre Dame Bookstore to find presents for us all.

I also have a couple of books my father inscribed and gave to my mother. In T. S. Eliot's *Notes Towards the Definition of Culture*, he wrote, *To my beloved wife / Xmas 1961/ DPK*. So many thoughts arise when I read this inscription: that my mother loved T. S. Eliot all her life; that my father signed off as "DPK" even on love notes to his wife; that part of what drew my parents together was their mutual love of literature; that their first and only child had died the previous March, yet they somehow found a way to celebrate Christmas that year. Forty years later, my dad gave my mom *The Unknown Sigrid Undset: Jenny and Other Works* for Christmas. His inscription reads, *To the love of my life / Merry Xmas, Nan / Dec. 25, 01 / Don*. Sigrid Undset remained a touchstone for my parents all their lives. I treasure these books not only for the brilliant words inside but for the love—and love of literature—they symbolize. I suspect there are other such books I'll come across and that my parents will continue to make themselves felt in this way. In fact, it's already happened.

I've mentioned that my husband and I culled books in our move from a house to an apartment. Going through our books again one day as we were preparing to pack, I pulled *The Lost Painting: The Quest for a Caravaggio Masterpiece*, by Jonathan Harr, off the shelf. I showed it to Paul. "Do you want to keep this?" I asked. "It's not mine," he said. "Well, it's not mine," I replied, and then I opened it. Seeing the price-clipped dustjacket, I knew what awaited me, and there it was: *Merry Christmas, Kristin / from Mom and Dad / Love.* I'd forgotten I even had it. A few weeks before that, I opened a small art book called *Van Gogh in St. Rémy und Auvers: Gemälde 1889/1890*, by Uwe M. Schneede, and saw another inscription from my mother, this one wishing me a Merry Christmas in German.

In learning to cope with loss, I'm also trying to set aside the mental images that continually arise of my parents in their declining years. I want to focus more on the good times, when they were healthy and vibrant. Paul helps with that, repeating strange or silly things they said and reminding me of funny incidents, like when my dad climbed a ladder and nailed a rubber snake to the side of the house to ward off woodpeckers. I think of his favorite *Far Side* cartoon, where a cat puts a coin in a gumball machine full of mice, and one of them shouts, "Randy's goin' down!" I think of my mother laughing uproariously throughout *Cabin Boy* while Paul and I looked on in amazement, and trips to Seattle when she, my sister, and I had leisurely lunches at Café Campagne after browsing around Pike Place Market. There are so many happy times to recall along with their last few years—and even those had moments of beauty and grace, not just sickness and sorrow.

And you, holding this book in your hands, nearing its end. Perhaps you'll read one of the books I wrote about that sparked your interest. Maybe you'll be prompted to peruse your own shelves for books with inscriptions from your parents or other loved ones. Maybe you'll make sure to ask them all the questions before it's too late. Or watch your dad's favorite movie with him, even if you fear it might be boring. And stay on the phone with your mom for as long as you can, even though she tells you the same stories over and over. Do it for their sake and for yours when they're no longer here, when the world feels off-kilter and like it will never right itself again. Maybe in time, it will. TAMÁM.

Complete List of
Inscribed Books

A Light in the Attic, by Shel Silverstein

> To Kristin
> with all our love
> Merry Christmas!
> 1981

A Child's Christmas in Wales, by Dylan Thomas
Christmas 1982

> To Kristin –
> A wonderful Christmas
> story by a great poet.
> Love,
> Mother and Dad

Brontë Sisters: *Wuthering Heights* and *Jane Eyre*

> To Kristin,
> for her 14th Christmas
> Read with delight and
> pleasure, my dear.
> Love, forever and
> ever,
> Dad 1983

Collected Poems of Emily Dickinson

> Merry Christmas to Kristin
> from Mother and Dad – 1984
> We hope you learn to love
> these poems by America's
> greatest woman poet.

The Complete Illustrated Works of Lewis Carroll

> To Kristin
> from Mother and
> Dad – Xmas, 1985
> Enjoy!

Rubáiyát of Omar Khayyám, Rendered into English verse by Edward Fitzgerald

> Dear Kristin,
> I think 17 is the
> Perfect age to read this.
> I hope you love it.
> Love on Christmas,
> Mother
> 1986

William Trevor: The Collected Stories

> Merry Christmas, Honey
> from
> Mom and Dad
> 1993

The New Basics Cookbook, by Julee Rosso and Sheila Lukins

> Dear Kristin,
> Good cookin'!
> Merry Christmas 1993

Van Gogh in St. Rémy und Auvers: Gemälde 1889/1890, by Uwe M. Schneede

> To Kristin
> Fröhliche Weinachten!
> Love,
> Mom
> 1994

Chaucer and His England, by G.G. Coulton

> 9/22/95
> Happy birthday,
> Kristin
> from Mom

Reading in the Dark, by Seamus Deane

> Christmas 1997
> To Kristin
> from Mom

The Life and Works of Munch, by Amanda O'Neill

> To Kristin
> from Mom
> Happy Birthday!
> All my love
> 1998

The Love of a Good Woman, by Alice Munro

> To Kristin
> from Mom
> Merry Christmas, 1998

Iris Murdoch: A Life, by Peter J. Conradi

> Dear Kristin,
> We can take a hint!
> Merry Christmas and
> Love
> Mom and Dad

Bloomsbury at Home, by Pamela Todd

> 2002
> Merry Christmas, Kristin
> When will they stop publishing
> about them?
> Love,
> Mom

When the Trees Say Nothing, by Thomas Merton

> Kristin:
> Get to know Thomas
> Merton, the greatest spiritual
> writer of the
> 20th century.
> Happy Christmas,
> Dad

The Lost Painting: The Quest for a Caravaggio Masterpiece, by Jonathan Harr

> Merry Christmas, Kristin
> from Mom and Dad
> Love

A Bit on the Side: Stories, by William Trevor

> September 22, 2006
> Kristin, You should be able to

find a few laughs in here!
Love from Mom

Seeing, by José Saramago

9/22/06
Happy Birthday, Kristin
from Mom with love

The Mrs. Dalloway Reader

September 22, 2006

Leonard Woolf, A Biography, by Victoria Glendinning

Merry Christmas
to Kristin
from Mom
2006

The Ode Less Travelled: Unlocking the Poet Within, by Stephen Fry

To Kristin –   2006
Merry Christmas
from Mom

A Good Man is Hard to Find and Other Stories, by Flannery
O'Connor

Kristin:
F. O'Connor and
Thomas Merton are
two authors who have
influenced me greatly.
Hope they do the same
for you.
Love,
Dad
Merry Xmas 2006

Shakespeare, *The Sonnets*

> Christmas 2007
> Kristin,
> I hope you enjoy reading
> these. Also, <u>memorize</u> <u>them</u>.
> Love from Mom

Mrs. Woolf and the Servants: An Intimate History of Domestic Life in Bloomsbury, by Alison Light

> 9/22/2008
> Dear Kristin,
> Congratulations on your 38th [sic]
> birthday.
> I hope you enjoy this book
> about an insufferable snob.
> Love,
> Mom

When Everything Changed: The Amazing Journey of American Women from 1960 to the Present, by Gail Collins

> Christmas 2009
> Kristin,
> This book is important. You all
> need to know what the past –
> during my lifetime – was like
> and the hard work that
> lies behind your privileges
> today.
> Love,
> Mom

Luka and the Fire of Life, by Salman Rushdie
> Merry Christmas, 2010
> Kristin from
> Mom and Dad - love

Bibliography

Preface

Lutz, Deborah. *The Brontë Cabinet: Three Lives in Nine Objects.* W. W. Norton, 2015.

Woolf, Virginia. *A Room of One's Own.* 1929. Annotated and with an introduction by Susan Gubar. Gen. Ed. Mark Hussey. Harcourt, 2005.

Chapter 1

Eliot, T. S. "The Love Song of J. Alfred Prufrock." *Poetry Foundation.* https://www.poetryfoundation.org/poetrymagazine/poems/44212/the-love-song-of-j-alfred-prufrock

Oliver, Mary. "The Summer Day." *Library of Congress.* https://www.loc.gov/programs/poetry-and-literature/poet-laureate/poet-laureate-projects/poetry-180/all-poems/item/poetry-180-133/the-summer-day/

Silverstein, Shel. *A Light in the Attic.* Harper & Row, 1981.

Chapter 2

Kindt, Julia. "On Nostalgia." *Meanjin Quarterly*, Winter 2018. https://meanjin.com.au/essays/on-nostalgia/

Joyce, James. "The Dead." *The Literature Network.* https://www.online-literature.com/james_joyce/958/

Sweeney, Paula. "Nostalgia Reconsidered." *Ratio: An International Journal of Analytic Philosophy*, 21 June 2020. https://onlinelibrary.wiley.com/doi/full/10.1111/rati.12272

Thomas, Dylan. *A Child's Christmas in Wales.* Illustrated by Edward Ardizzone. David R. Godine, 1980.

Chapter 3
Browne, Harry. *Frontman: Bono (In the Name of Power)*. Verso, 2013.
Deane, Seamus. *Reading in the Dark*. Knopf, 1996.
"Faul, Denis." *Wikipedia*. Last updated 18 Dec. 2020. https://
en.wikipedia.org/wiki/Denis_Faul
Heaney, Seamus. "Whatever You Say, Say Nothing." *100 Poems*.
Farrar, Straus and Giroux, 2020.
"More IRA Posters Plastered on International Wall in West Bel-
fast." *Irish News*, 26 April 2016. https://www.irishnews.com/
news/2016/04/26/news/more-ira-posters-plastered-on-interna-
tional-wall-in-west-belfast-498419/
Woolf, Virginia. *A Room of One's Own*. 1929. Annotated and
with an introduction by Susan Gubar. Gen. Ed. Mark Hussey.
Harcourt, 2005.

Chapter 4
Bodette, Melody, and Mitch Wertlieb. "Salmon Rushdie on Fiction,
Religion and Freedom of Expression." *Vermont Public Radio*, 15
Jan. 2015. https://www.vermontpublic.org/vpr-news/2015-01-15/
salman-rushdie-on-fiction-religion-and-freedom-of-expression
Rushdie, Salman. *Luka and the Fire of Life*. Random House, 2010.
---. *Haroun and the Sea of Stories*. Granta, 1990.

Chapter 5
Ahmed, Sara. *Living a Feminist Life*. Duke UP, 2017.
Davis, Angela. *Women, Race & Class*. Vintage, 1983.
Light, Alison. *Mrs. Woolf and the Servants: An Imtimate History
of Domestic Life in Bloomsbury*. Bloomsbury, 2008.

Chapter 6
Giovanni, Nikki. "Allowables." *Get Lit Anthology,* 2013. https://
getlitanthology.org/poemdetail/125/
Jacobs, Alan. "Thomas Merton: The Monk Who Became a Prophet." *The New Yorker*, 18 Dec. 2018. https://www.newyorker.
com/books/under-review/thomas-merton-the-monk-who-be-
came-a-prophet
Merton, Thomas. *When the Trees Say Nothing: Writings on Nature*.
Ed. Kathleen Deignan. Sorin Books, 2003.

Chapter 7

Angier, Carole. *Jean Rhys: Life and Work*. Little, Brown and Company, 1990.

Brontë, Emily, and Charlotte Brontë. *The Brontë Sisters: Wuthering Heights, Jane Eyre*. Longmeadow Press, 1983.

Carson, Anne. *Glass, Irony & God*. New Directions, 1992.

---. *Plainwater*. Vintage, 2000.

Czarnecki, Kristin. *The First Kristin: The Story of a Naming*. Main Street Rag, 2020.

Minick, Jeff. "Brontë Sisters Part and Parcel of the Magic of Haworth." *Smoky Mountain News*, 24 June 2015. https://smoky-mountainnews.com/archives/item/15933-bronte-sisters-part-and-parcel-of-the-magic-of-haworth

Morrison, Blake. "The Rise and Rise of Brontëmania." *The Guardian*, 9 Sep. 2011. https://www.theguardian.com/books/2011/sep/09/charlotte-bronte-jane-eyre

Orlean, Susan. *The Library Book*. Simon & Schuster, 2018.

Plath, Sylvia. "Wuthering Heights." *The Collected Poems of Sylvia Plath*. Harper & Row, 1981.

Seymour, Miranda. *I Used to Live Here Once: The Haunted Life of Jean Rhys*. William Collins, 2022.

Shulevitz, Judith. "The Secret of Charlotte, Emily, and Anne Brontë." *The Atlantic*, 15 June 2016. https://www.theatlantic.com/magazine/archive/2016/06/the-brontes-secret/480726/

Temple, Emily. "Apparently the Brontës all died so early because they spent their lives drinking graveyard water." *LitHub*, 14 May 2021. https://lithub.com/apparently-the-brontes-all-died-so-early-because-they-spent-their-lives-drinking-graveyard-water/

Woolf, Virginia. "Haworth, November 1904." *The Guardian*. 21 Dec. 1904. https://digital.library.upenn.edu/women/woolf/VW-Bronte.html

---. "*Jane Eyre* and *Wuthering Heights*." *Collected Essays, Volume 1*. Harcourt, Brace & World, 1967.

---. *The Letters of Virginia Woolf, Volume One, 1888-1912*. Ed. Nigel Nicolson and Joanne Trautmann. Harcourt Brace Jovanovich, 1975.

---. *A Room of One's Own*. 1929. Annotated and with an Introduction by Susan Gubar. Gen. Ed. Mark Hussey. Harcourt, 2005.

---. *To the Lighthouse*. 1927. Annotated and with an Introduction by Mark Hussey. Harcourt, 2005.

Chapter 8

Morrison, Toni. *Jazz*. Vintage, 1992.

Munro, Alice. *The Love of a Good Woman: Stories*. Knopf, 1998.

Chapter 9

Ahmed, Sara. *Living a Feminist Life*. Duke UP, 2017.

Collins, Gail. *When Everything Changed: The Amazing Journey of American Women from 1960 to the Present*. Little, Brown and Company, 2009.

Gay, Roxane. *Bad Feminist*. Harper, 2014.

Chapter 10

Cash, Jean W. *Flannery O'Connor: A Life*. University of Tennessee Press, 2002.

Munro, Alice. *The Love of a Good Woman: Stories*. Knopf, 1998.

O'Connor, Flannery. *A Good Man is Hard to Find and Other Stories*. Harvest, 1981.

Chapter 11

Black, Julia. "I Thought Cooking Would Make Me a Bad Feminist." *Bon Appetit*, 18 Oct. 2017. https://www.bonappetit.com/story/cooking-bad-feminist

Chozick, Amy. "Hillary Clinton and the Return of the (Unbaked) Cookies." *The New York Times*, 5 Nov. 2016. https://www.nytimes.com/2016/11/06/us/politics/hillary-clinton-cookies.html

Clark, Heather. *Red Comet: The Short Life and Blazing Art of Sylvia Plath*. Penguin, 2020.

Lutz, Deborah. *The Brontë Cabinet: Three Lives in Nine Objects*. W. W. Norton, 2015.

Martyris, Nina. "How Suffragists Used Cookbooks as a Recipe for Subversion." *The Salt—NPR*, 5 Nov. 2015. https://www.npr.org/sections/thesalt/2015/11/05/454246666/how-suffragists-used-cookbooks-as-a-recipe-for-subversion

Mishra, Akanksha. "Cook Thy Meal, Love Thy Body. Why I am a Feminist Who Cooks." *Feminism in India*, 19 Oct. 2018. https://feminisminindia.com/2018/10/19/feminist-love-cook/#:~:text=I%20cook%20because%20as%20a,on%20human%20bodies%20and%20desires.

Rosso, Julee, and Sheila Lukins. *The New Basics Cookbook*. Workman, 1989.

Sharma, Aurvi. "I Rejected Cooking in the Name of Feminism—Until I Had To." *Bon Appetit*, 6 Jan. 2021. https://www.bonappetit.com/story/rejected-cooking-for-feminism

Chapter 12

Arnold, Matthew. "Dover Beach." *Poetry Foundation*. https://www.poetryfoundation.org/poems/43588/dover-beach

Bird, Laura Anne. "On Buying Too Many Books." 21 Dec. 2021. *Laura Bird Books*. https://www.laurabirdbooks.com/post/on-buying-too-many-books#:~:text=There%20will%20never%20be%20a,books%20back%20to%20the%20library.

Fitzgerald, Edmund, Trans. *Rubáiyát of Omar Khayyám*. Weathervane Books, 1985.

Marvell, Andrew. "To His Coy Mistress." *Poetry Foundation*. https://www.poetryfoundation.org/poems/44688/to-his-coy-mistress

Oliver, Mary. "The Summer Day." *Library of Congress*. https://www.loc.gov/programs/poetry-and-literature/poet-laureate/poet-laureate-projects/poetry-180/all-poems/item/poetry-180-133/the-summer-day/

"Omar Khayyám—Biography, Facts, and Pictures." *Famous Scientists*. https://www.famousscientists.org/omar-khayyam/

"The Rubáiyát of Omar Khayyám of Naishapur." *GradeSaver.com*. https://www.gradesaver.com/the-rubaiyat-of-omar-khayyam-of-naishapur

Selina, Howard. "Tony Selina Obituary." *The Guardian*, 25 Nov. 2015. https://www.theguardian.com/artanddesign/2015/nov/25/tony-selina-obituary

Woolf, Virginia. *To the Lighthouse*. 1927. Annotated and with an Introduction by Mark Hussey. Harcourt, 2005.

Afterword

Czarnecki, Kristin. "Expressing the Inexpressible." *Peatsmoke: A Literary Journal*, 12 March 2021. https://www.peatsmokejournal.com/spring-2021-nonfiction/kristin-czarnecki

Lutz, Deborah. *The Brontë Cabinet: Three Lives in Nine Objects*. W. W. Norton, 2015.

Rilke, Rainer Maria. *The Dark Interval: Letters on Loss, Grief, and Transformation*. Ed. and Trans. Ulrich Baer. Modern Library, 2018.

Woolf, Virginia. *A Room of One's Own*. 1929. Annotated and with an Introduction by Susan Gubar. Gen. Ed. Mark Hussey. Harcourt, 2005.

Acknowledgements

Permissions

Chapter 3 was published as "When Reading in the Dark Turns on the Light: How Inscriptions Brought Ireland to Indiana" in April 2022 in *The Smart Set* and is reprinted with permission.

Chapter 6 was published as "Beckonings from the Bookshelf" in March 2022 in *The Porch Magazine* and is reprinted with permission.

Chapter 7 was published as "Braving the Brontës" in March 2023 in *Masque & Spectacle* and is reprinted with permission.

Gratitude

Heartfelt thanks to Jodie Toohey for giving this book the perfect home at Legacy Book Press.

To my sister, Cynthia Jordan, and my brother, Ted Kommers, first readers of all my writing about our family.

To my writing crew and all those who provided feedback along the way: Emma Bolden, Barbara Burch, Erica Delsandro, Kelcey Ervick, Sinane Goulet, Catherine Hollis, Erin Kingsley, Annie MacConnel, Mia Martin, Molly McCaffrey, Cece Mast McTigue, Megan Quigley, and Carrie Rohman.

Eternal love and gratitude to Nancy and Donald Kommers for filling our family home with love and literature.

Above all, my love and thanks to Paul for making our dreams come true. *Viva San Pietro!*

About the Author

Kristin Czarnecki is the author of a memoir, *The First Kristin: The Story of a Naming*, and a chapbook, *Sliced*. She has published creative nonfiction, poetry, literary criticism, and book reviews in a variety of venues.

She lives in Gloucester, Massachusetts.

www.ingramcontent.com/pod-product-compliance
Lightning Source LLC
Chambersburg PA
CBHW050856150626
46549CB00013B/2336